A Chance to Tell

A Chance to Tell

by

Wilbert Smikle

DORRANCE PUBLISHING CO., INC.
PITTSBURGH, PENNSYLVANIA 15222

The events, people, and places herein are depicted to the best recollection of the author, who assumes complete and sole responsibility for the accuracy of this narrative.

ISBN: 978-1-4349-0078-4
Library of Congress Control Number: 2008922800

Printed in the United States of America

First Printing

For more information or to order additional books, please contact:
Dorrance Publishing Co., Inc.
701 Smithfield Street
Pittsburgh, Pennsylvania 15222
U.S.A.
1-800-788-7654
www.dorrancebookstore.com

Dedication

This book is dedicated to my autistic daughter, Chaina Ellen Smikle, whom I have cared for since birth and will continue my last years, to her benefit, Father Wilbert Smikle.

Contents

Prologue ix

Preface xi

Acknowledgments xvii

The Dental Group xix

Introduction xxiii

The Dramatization 1

A Chance to Tell the Story 12

The Dreams 33

Retirement 94

Estelle and Wilbert 95

Family Reunion 96

Conclusion 100

Glossary 101

Prologue

After retiring, I found that the air in Jamaica relieved my breathing discomfort caused by hazardous job conditions. I therefore spent most of my time in Jamaica. The house I built in Davyton is one of several locations where I can be found on the Island. It is also the oasis of the Dental team as they continue to offer their services twice yearly under the leadership of the EDS Dental Group, Dr. Johnson, and associates Gene Scott, Brad Rostad, and others.

Preface

The autobiography of Wilbert Smikle is an interesting account of the life and experiences of a Jamaican boy growing up on the island of Jamaica and ending up in America. He represents an example of how a productive young man growing up in the Caribbean in the twentieth century experienced many challenges as a result of his movement from Jamaica to England and then to America. Family, church, and many contacts helped him to find a path of survival. His marriage and church affiliation in America led to a productive life. He returned home to Jamaica and shared his experiences by giving back to the area in which he grew up. He supplied resources, time, and dedication to education of youth and help for those in need. Wilbert's life represents what a person coming out of the non-western world should look like when progress and development in the third world call on their own sons to give back to their homeland so that the present generation there can progress.

Dr. Leonard Bethel
Professor
Rutgers University
New Brunswick, N.J. USA.

A Chance to Tell.

Congratulations to Wilbert Smikle on the publication of his first book.

His vision of the future came true, as his book of his memoirs relates. Not many a Jamaican of humble beginnings can claim this reality, nor, indeed, can write and have the book published about it. Apart from being a confident person, and a devout Christian, Mr. Wilbert Smikle, is a man for the people, for his family, for the Church. The publication of this autobiography could be the crowning achievement of this suave but friendly and hospitable old-time Jamaican gentleman who makes and opens the way for the next Jamaican who is helping him/herself to succeed. I know this to be true, as my own family is only one of the many who owe much to his benevolence.

May this autobriography, "A Chance To Tell", a record of events in our Jamaican generations to come.

Auma T. Folkes, Ed.D.
Assistant Professor
Department of Teacher Education
Northern Caribbean University
Mandeville, Jamaican W.I.
14ᵗʰ March, 2008

A Chance to Tell.

Give Wilbert Smikle (or—Mas Wilbert) a "chance to tell" his story. Written in simple, straightforward language, it is a compelling account of how one man's boyhood dreams became reality. Journey with Wilbert Smikle from the most humble condition in the remote mountains of Jamaica to the big cities of the eastern seaboard. Wherever he has gone, his life had left an indelible mark on the lives of people across the social stratum.

Relentlessly tenacious and plodding. Wilbert never gave up—nor did he forget those less fortunate—or "where he came from." Hence our paths crossed when he returned to his homeland of Jamaica, where my family and I have served as missionaries over the last twenty years. He unashamedly gives God credit for his "life of good fortune." More than being "in the right place at the right time" Wilbert believes his life has been "divinely orchestrated." This is a human success story of the best order. Read and enjoy! Give Wilbert a "chance to tell" his story and share in his triumph!

Rev. Brad Rostad
Directore—Christ the Cornerstone Mission
Missionary—Jamaica.

A Chance to Tel.

Wilbert Smilke's autobiography is an extraordinary, yet humble life adventure written with complete frankness, candidness and honest self exposure.

Dr. Lisa Wagner.
Dentist — Atlanta, Georgia.

A Chance to Tell.

This book is a testament to Wilbert Smikle's character and commitment. Though his life travels have taken him to England, Canada and America and beyond, yet he has never left behind his beloved birthplace—Jamaica.

> *Gene Scott.*
> *Real Estate Developer—Atlanta, Georgia.*
> *Director of Dental Ministry—Jamaica.*

Acknowledgments

It is with love that I express remembrance of my parents Joseph and Ellen Smikle for bringing me up in the way of the Lord.

To my brothers and sisters, thanks for your love and respect, especially David, who was my constant companion in my youth.

To Dr. Auma Tess Folkes and Reverend Folkes for their spiritual advise.

To Merritt Kerr, Alfred Williams, Howard Hall, Joseph Robinson, and John Smith for their genuine warmth and loving friendship.

To my late wife, Estelle, whose love, support, and dedication gave me strength to fight for a better life.

To the leaders of the Dental Group from Atlanta: Gene Scott, Brad Rostad, and all those doctors who have been giving voluntary dental services to the needy school children and adults for many years. Also to Tommy, the wife of Dr. Johnson, whose vision of an interview of my life gave me the courage "to take a chance."

To the former Governor General of Jamaica, His Excellency Sir Howard Cooke, who graciously stopped at the Davyton House and extended thanks to me for allowing the dental group to use my home during their voluntary service to the community.

To my grandson, who used his computer savvy to help me with the photos and graphics.

The Dental Group

Dental Group

10th August, 1993.

Dear Mr. Smikle,

     I thank you for your letter of July 29, 1993. I do wish to congratulate you for all that you are doing to improve the Davyton Community.

     The project to create a situation in which visitors can be made comfortable is a very laudable one. The proximity of the house to the Davyton Church will provide accommodation for missionaries and other persons who wish to help in the cause of Christ.

     I thank you for the photographs that you have sent as they will help me to identify what the project is all about.

     God's willing I shall be at Davyton United Church on August 29, 1993. As I would like to shake hands with you I ask that you identify yourself.

     Once again let me congratulate you for your effort and may you be inspired to continue to work for The Master.

Sincerely,

H. Cooke

Governor-General

Mr. Wilbert Smikle

Davyton United Church, 150th Anniversary, 1993

Introduction

"Who is that man?"

The question was directed to the sergeant of a local police station, located two miles from Davyton, the scene of an unusual occurrence, by the Chief of police and law enforcement in Mandeville, the capital of Manchester, on the morning of August 30, 1993. At the age of 68, I was fortunate in purchasing the Haynes property. During my youth I spent most of my cherished moments on this property. Three years later, I built a home and called it "The Davyton House."

A missionary dental team from Atlanta, Georgia, offered free dental care to the needy school children and adults in the area and requested the use of a section of the house for lodging and storing of vital dental equipment. Realizing the importance of their service to the community, I allowed them the use of the house.

News of their services to the island reached the attention of one of the most important officials, His Excellency, The Governor General Sir Howard Cooke. On a special mission in the area, he stopped at the Davyton House and extended his gratitude and appreciation to me for allowing the team the use of the property.

As I was unknown to the officials, and my name was not recorded among the list of dignitaries, eyebrows were raised over the impromptu stop by the Governor General.

An order was issued August 30 by the inspector to secretly investigate the occasion and ascertain my identity and the relevancy of the impromptu visit by the Governor General.

As a youth, and one of nine children, I worked on the family farm and was allowed only limited time in school. During those school days, I seldom missed interaction with schoolmates and social activities. After graduation I attended a government sponsored practical training center for boys, where I spent three years studying agriculture and woodworking. My ambition was to improve the family standard of living by working and making a financial contribution.

Before the end of my training I had five dreams, which took me to locations unknown to me. At the fulfillment of each of the first three dreams, I sang in reverence the same melody, but with different lyrics, for each location. It was a joyful expression seeing "God's acts come true."

During World War II, at the age of twenty-four, I was among several thousand men sponsored by the United States War Food Administration (WFA) to work on agricultural farms and in industries from 1943–1945.

My life story is one of contrast, as it covers three countries: Jamaica, the place of my birth, which has a class system under colonialism; the United States during World War II, where discrimination and segregation were placed on hold in the supreme "effort for victory"; and England, after the war, where discrimination and segregation were not in practice, and people hugged and greeted everyone, regardless of race or color.

Returning to the United States in 1948, the tolerance that had existed during World War II was put aside, and discrimination and segregation were quite evident, as in years before the war. I found a job where about 5 percent of the 2500 or more employees were black. Equality and job promotions were reserved for whites, and very little consideration was given to the promotion of blacks.

My personal goal to break down the barriers and reach the top took several years. This was accomplished with the help of new civil right laws and a change of my attitude to one of humility through "Devine guidance." I supported the civil rights movement and the great leaders by raising funds. The joy of giving towards my youthful commitment gave me great satisfaction.

This writing is an acknowledgement of God's Devine guidance in my life, and to tell you that you can be lifted up, wherever you are, by His power. It also tells you that a humble youth born in the hills of Davyton, unknown, though many deeds of kindness done, would not be known had it not been that act of gratitude expressed by His Excellency Sir Howard Cooke, Governor General of Jamaica, on August 29, 1993.

Dates and incidents cited are taken from My Farm Worker's Diary.

Disclaimer

The names of some characters involved in "The Dramatization" may have been changed for dramatic effect and to protect the innocent. Any resemblance to real persons, living or dead, is purely coincidental.

The wife of a prominent law enforcement official was infuriated when she learned that they had missed a large church ceremony involving His Excellency the Governor General of the Island. Her husband was indignant due to the failure of communication when he was not notified by the superiors of the impending visit of the Governor General.

Adherence to protocol failed when His Excellency made an impromptu stop at the home of a man, unknown to the legal authorities. The question of "Who is that man?" and the significance of finding out took precedence over their humiliation. A plot was planned and dramatized to secretly ascertain the answer..

The Dramatization

It was early Monday morning on August 30, 1993, when inspector Robert McPherson overheard his wife, Marlene, in a telephone conversation.

"You seem a bit upset darling, what was it all about?"

"Well, Robert, you may think it's gossiping, but I am really furious."

"Sure, Marlene, but I heard my name mentioned. Why was my name involved? I would like to know."

"Why it is that you never mentioned to me that the Governor General was right here in your jurisdiction yesterday? Most of the so-called who's who knew of the occasion. I just happened to call my friend Louise for a recipe, and before I could explain my request, she wanted to know why we were not at the affair at the Davyton Church yesterday evening. I was certainly shocked to think that she knew about it in advance and never mentioned a word to me. I am humiliated. I really don't like to miss these affairs. I am hurt that you had not mentioned this to me."

"Darling," said the inspector.

"Don't darling me, "Marlene snapped, "this is not the time for romance. And to think that Louise, whom I *thought* to be my friend, knew about it and never even mentioned a word to me. And that half-pint husband of hers is really giving me the creeps with his foxy grin. They both make me sick."

"Alright dear," said the inspector, "this whole matter is news to me. I knew nothing about it. Anyhow, tell me more so that I can get to the root of everything that happened."

"Well, Robert, the Davyton United Church of Jamaica had their 150th anniversary, and the Governor General was the guest speaker. All the dignitaries in the community were there. Six churches, with their choirs and Sunday school children, joined the parade that escorted the Governor General's procession from a quarter of a mile down the road to the church ground, singing and carrying flowers as they slowly marched toward the entrance of the church. I heard that the Governor General gave a very touching sermon, and I will *never* forgive Louise."

"Well, Marlene, as you know, we have just recently been transferred to this location, but that was no reason not to be notified by the authorities."

"Yes, Robert, I agree. Anyhow, Louise said that on their way home they had to wait in traffic for almost thirty minutes because the Governor General had his limousine detour into this man's driveway, and he entered into his house. The motorcycle escort and the news media were far ahead and did not know that the Governor General had made an impromptu stop. Traffic was backed up all over the place. The escort stopped all traffic and everyone had to wait until the procession ended. The fact that the news media and escort were so far ahead leads me to believe that it will not be on the television or in the newspapers tomorrow."

"Alright, Marlene, they caught me off guard this time, but I will get to the bottom of this. I am going to the office right away. Please calm yourself down, and by the way, please make sure that the recipe that you called Louise for is on the dinner table when I get home this evening."

With a short kiss, Inspector McPherson bid his wife adieu and headed towards his car, pondering over what he had heard and planning the best way to deal with the matter.

At the office, the inspector said, "Good morning, Miss Jones" with a saddened face to the secretary.

"Good morning, Inspector. You seem very sad today. Is anything wrong? It's such a lovely morning."

"Nothing really, Miss Jones, but you look so radiant this morning. I am sure it's from a beautiful weekend, and don't say no."

"Thank you, Inspector," answered Miss Jones, blushing, as she returned to her desk. "Please get my friend O'Grady on the phone. You can use his private line."

"Yes, Inspector," she replied.

While the phone was ringing, Inspector McPherson took a quick glance at the newspaper and was satisfied that nothing about the Davyton incident was mentioned.

After several rings, O'Grady answered. "Hello, McPherson. This has to be good news hearing from you so early. I was hoping it wasn't my wife; she always called to give news when arriving on the job in the morning. You know the prosecutor's office on a typical Monday morning; I have to listen with one ear just to give her peace of mind, and sometimes the old fellow is not up to it."

"Are you going to the gym today? This old hip is not what it used to be, you know, the constant up and down?"

"Well, Grady, I need the company. Will the usual time be OK?"

"Sure, Mack, that is fine with me"

"The Governor General was in the area yesterday at a church ceremony in a small district of Davyton."

"And you are telling me *after* the fact?" asked O'Grady. "You are certainly a friend."

"I observed while driving through the area last week that they were paving roads that have been neglected and cutting away low hanging tree limbs. I would love to have been there. I can imagine the motorcycle escort and the official limousines and all those people lining the roadway. Now tell me, where were you?"

McPherson hesitated for a while, then answered, "Someone neglected to inform me, but an unusual occurrence took place. On his return trip, the Governor General made an impromptu stop at the residence of someone unknown. He pulled into the driveway of this Davyton House and went inside."

"That doesn't seem to follow protocol," continued O'Grady.

"Do you know this man?" enquired McPherson.

"Well," said O'Grady, "I don't know of him, but it certainly would be a legal matter to find out. Just don't go about it legally. A secret, diplomatic way could bring the answer you need."

"Thank you, Grady, and make sure to listen to your wife with both ears. That peace of mind will be sweeter and more enjoyable." He hung up the phone and spoke to his secretary. "Miss Jones, please get me Sergeant Buxton of the Williamsfield station."

"Sure, Inspector."

Sergeant Buxton promptly picked up the phone after the second ring and identified himself.

"Yes, Sergeant Buxton, this is Miss Jones of the Inspector's office. The Inspector would like to speak with you. Please hold."

"Sergeant Buxton, good morning, how are you? How are things at your station and the surrounding areas?"

"Well, Inspector," said Sergeant Buxton. "Things have been quiet; no report of any incidents or wrongdoing."

"Very good," replied Inspector McPherson. "Now Buxton, let me get to my reason for calling you so early in the morning. An incident that occurred yesterday evening at the Davyton community, which is two miles from your station, just came to my attention. I was not aware that the Governor General was in the area and that he made an impromptu stop at the home of someone nobody seems to know. From now on I am asking for more cooperation from your department. The responsibility will be on your shoulders to inform me before and after any significant matter. Do I make myself clear?"

"Well, Inspector," said Buxton, "I am very sorry that you were not aware of the occasion."

"Yes, Buxton, but it would have been very embarrassing to my whole staff and me if any of my superiors had called regarding this matter."

"Yes, Inspector, I agree with your view point, but there has to be a good reason. I personally don't know this man, and the whole district is talking about it. The occasion was well covered by my station; Corporal William Brown, Detective John Williamson, and I were on hand, and everything went on smoothly. On the recessional, I was driving ahead of the motorcade and didn't realize that a stop had been made until the traffic started to back up and congest the road. Horns started blowing; it lasted about thirty minutes, but after that, everything was normal."

"Now Buxton, I want to be fully informed about this gentleman and the possible reason for the impromptu visit of the Governor General. In my jurisdiction we are responsible for every official affair. We will work as a team and I demand that everything at my command will be made possible and that cooperation and coordination be achieved. All members under my command must be alerted. Things went smoothly yesterday evening, yet one never knows where evil lurks. I don't know this man at Davyton, but I would like to share any good thought that the Governor General has about him. We may be missing something good right under our noses. As you know, protocol *must* be observed."

"Yes, Inspector, Good reasoning."

"Now Buxton, I will be sending my chief detective, John McGuire, to you within the next two hours. Get a corporal from your station that is familiar with the Davyton district. Take both men with you and immediately proceed to Davyton and find out everything possible about this man. McGuire will report to me directly. No one should be told of our reason for this unusual visit. Be careful to keep the news media out. Bear in mind that the Governor General should have no idea of this mission because it may stir concern or cause embarrassment to me. I am asking you gentlemen to dress casual, no uniform. Give this gentleman all the respect that will make him comfortable and in a pleasant mood to talk. There should be no secret taping."

"Yes, Inspector, I remember what taping did to President Dixon."

"No, Buxton, *Nixon!* It actually chased him out of the white castle."

"Yes, Inspector, I see you really remember history," said Buxton.

"Try to make him think that your superior extends a cordial expression of gratitude. Well, that is all for now, Buxton."

"Thank you, Inspector."

"Oh, by the way, give that beautiful wife of yours a nice hello from Marlene and me."

At Williamsfield station, Sergeant Buxton was burning with anger. "I can't blame the Inspector, but how did he find out so much in such a short time?" he grumbled to himself. "This is a free country, but there are too many watchdogs." As he continued to grumble, he noticed Corporal Brown standing at the door.

"What's happening, Sarge? You seem to be talking to yourself."

"Please close the door and have a seat," said Sergeant Buxton.

"Yes sir," said the Corporal.

"Listen Brown, Detective McGuire from the Inspector's office will be here shortly, and we will be taking a trip to Davyton."

"A joy ride, Sarge?"

"No," said the Sergeant, "we will be visiting a gentleman by the name of Smikle. Just a courtesy call from the Inspector's office."

"Can you give me more details?" asked Brown.

"The only prominent person up there is the Minister of the church, and everybody knows him. But the Governor General stopped at Mr. Smikle's home, The Davyton House."

"Hey Sarge, a car just pulled up. It's Detective McGuire. Just take a look at the car he is driving, a brand new Toyota Camry."

Sergeant Buxton took a curious look and said, "Oh, yes, that's Inspector McPherson's personal vehicle. I have seen his wife driving it from time to time."

McGuire knocked, then opened the door, stretched out his hand, and said, "Good morning, Sergeant Buxton."

The sergeant rose from his seat and said with a smile, "Hello, McGuire." He turned and nodded to Corporal Brown and said, "You've met Corporal Brown, haven't you?"

"Oh yes," said the detective as he shook Corporal Brown's hand.

Sergeant Buxton, with a slight grin, said, "Hey McGuire, brand new car *and* a brand new suit. You are looking so sharp and crisp."

"Yes, Sarge," said McGuire, "Inspector's orders. The last time I wore a tie was when I tied the knot—you know, when I got married. Anyhow, Inspector wants us to dress casual, no uniform. He's concerned that all of the district people will gather around, thinking that we are investigating a big case, and he doesn't want to create a crowd, and I agree with him."

Corporal Brown grunted, "Well, I don't have a suit."

"What about the one you have hanging in the closet?"

"No, not good enough, it needs pressing."

Sergeant Buxton asked McGuire, "Why is it that Inspector McPherson allowed his personal vehicle to be used for this occasion?"

"Well," said McGuire, "My vehicle is old and in the mechanic's shop. Inspector thinks the government Jeep is too familiar in the area; everyone knows the license plate and will assemble at the gate of the Smikle's residence with curiosity. But with this car, there will be no suspicion. I am quite sure you will enjoy the ride. He wants us to act as friends to the Smikle family. Corporal Brown, you've been a Romeo in the area; no doubt you may know more about this gentleman." I have discovered a few things from my insider. There are two Smikles in the area, one of them is very prosperous and a very good farmer who employs quite a few people and is well known for his generosity."

"Yes," said Corporal Brown, "His name is David and they call him 'The Phantom'—and he really looks like one."

"Well," said Sergeant Buxton, "we want to be sure we have the right person."

"Yes sir," said Brown, "the other Smikle has just recently moved into the area and built a new house; very little is known about him. The house has a wide driveway and a very large gate. It's the only building with a driveway wide enough for the Governor General's limousine to enter without problem, and the building is a very attractive one with the flag on the gate post."

"Flag on the gate post?" inquired Sergeant Buxton,

"Yes, sir" said Corporal Brown.

"What kind of flag?" asked Detective McGuire.

"Our national flag," said Brown, "And no other building in the area has a flag so visible for all to see."

"Oh yes, I remember seeing that flag yesterday," said Sergeant Buxton. "Gentlemen, allow me to be the spokesperson when we get there. I believe, with a little enthusiasm from both of you, we will be able to find out who this man *really* is. Let's hope that he is at home, and remember, not a word of this matter to anyone. We will give him all the respect and honor that is due to a prince. Now, whatever I say, you gentlemen are to add a compliment or two."

"What do you mean?" asked Corporal Brown.

McGuire tried to explain by saying, "Well, Brown, what the sergeant means is quite simple. For instance, if he says, 'beautiful flowers,' you are to say, 'lovely indeed' or 'beautiful roses.'"

"Yes," said Corporal Brown, "but suppose there are no roses?"

They were silent for a while until Sergeant Buxton announced, "Gentlemen, we are ready."

All three men went into the car, and as they proceeded, Sergeant Buxton remarked, "This is really a smooth riding car."

"Very smooth indeed," said Corporal Brown.

There was loud laughter from all three men as the understanding of "compliments" found its place, which made Sergeant Buxton very satisfied. "I notice the road is nicely repaired," said Sergeant Buxton.

"Yes sir," said Brown. "Every time someone of prominence from the government visits this area, the government always finds money to fix the roads. This time, they widened all the corners and fixed all the pot holes."

"Yes, I see," said Sergeant Buxton. "I remember two years ago when the mother of a Member of Parliament died and the funeral was at Davyton Church. The road was given the royal treatment."

"Yes," said Brown, "all the appeals that the people made for the government to fix the road after hurricane Gilbert fell on deaf ears, but as soon as one of their 'biggies' has to come this way, they always fork out thousands of dollars to make the roads as smooth as possible. We should be getting close. It is a new house on the right. We can't miss it. The name of the house is 'Davyton House' and it is written on the column of the gate."

As they continued, they saw the flag from a distance and saw the name as they approached.

"There it is," said Corporal Brown. The car stopped in front of the gate, and Corporal Brown was asked to ring the gate bell while McGuire and Sergeant Buxton remained quietly in the car.

Davyton House

The large gate stood like a fortress in front of the vehicle. Brown looked for the gate bell.

"Sarge," said Brown "there is no gate bell."

"Look, man, there is a car in the garage," answered McGuire.

Just then Corporal Brown picked up a small stone and knocked on the gate three times—then three more times.

My gardener, who was watering the roses and tall shrubberies on the far side of the building, and was not seen by the visitors, alerted me and requested permission to open the gate. Other members of my family thought the arrival of one of our expected friends was much earlier than anticipated. As I approached the gate, I realized the visitors were strangers.

Sergeant Buxton and Detective McGuire alighted from the car and walked towards me. "Mr. Smikle, I presume? Good morning, I am William Buxton."

"Good morning, gentlemen," I answered with curiosity. "Now tell me, to whom and for what occasion do I owe the honor of this visit?"

"Well sir, please meet my colleagues, Mr. Brown and Mr. McGuire. May we speak to you for a few minutes, sir?"

"Of course, follow me." As the men proceeded towards the steps, Sergeant Buxton said, "This is a lovely place."

"Lovely indeed," echoed Corporal Brown.

"Well, there is a lot of work to be done," I said.

"What is that beautiful flowery plant around the gate?" enquired McGuire.

"Oh," I said, "that is Bougainvillea."

"It is really beautiful," said Corporal Brown as the three men walked towards the door.

"This house has a lovely view; I can see Mandeville, which is seven miles away," said Detective McGuire.

"Oh yes," I said, "It is beautiful at night with all those lights in Mandeville; it's like a gallery of stars."

As they entered the living room, Sergeant Buxton apologized for the unannounced visit. "Mr. Smikle we are sorry to call on you so suddenly, but this is really a courtesy visit directed by our superior, Inspector Robert McPherson, from the Mandeville jurisdiction. I am Sergeant Buxton from the Williamsfield police station, and this is my assistant, Corporal William Brown. This other gentleman is the chief of detectives from the inspector's office in Mandeville, special Detective Mr. McGuire."

"Gentleman, is this really a courtesy call? What courtesy, may I ask?"

Sergeant Buxton looked at the other two officers, who gazed assuredly, with a smile. Then McGuire spoke, "Yes, Mr. Smikle, our superior, Inspector McPherson, would like to extend his personal appreciation to you for your generous hospitality towards the Governor General on his visit to you yesterday."

"Yes, Mr. Smikle," said Sergeant Buxton, "The news has reached his office, and this is his way of showing his superiors that he is active in everything that is important in his jurisdiction. As a matter of fact, he offered an apology for not coming with us today. Whenever someone does something good in the area, whether it is an officer or a private citizen, Mr. McPherson always extends some kind of acknowledgement. This also gives us the privilege to meet many of the distinguished citizens in the area, such as a man of your stature," said McGuire. "And may I ask how long you've known the Governor General?"

"Only for a short time," I answered. "Let's just say he is pleased with my assistance in helping the volunteer dental group from the US by letting them use this place as an oasis while giving their services freely to the needy school children and adults. He is a very religious man, you know, and encourages good actions."

"Oh Mr. Smikle," said Corporal Brown, "I've heard your voice in that lovely Davyton choir when I attend services."

"I've seen you many times, Corporal Brown. We need more male voices. It would be a privilege if you could join us. Do you gentlemen wish to enter your names in the guest book?"

"Yes sir," answered Sergeant Buxton. As they turned the pages, the signature of the Governor General caught their eyes. The three men glanced at each other in quiet assurance, that indeed, the Governor General had been a guest.

They looked keenly at the signature,

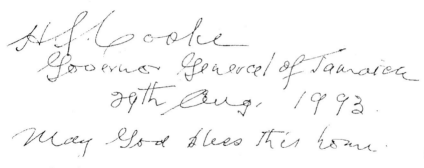

H.L. Cooke
Governor General of Jamaica
29th Aug. 1993.
May God bless this home.

Taken from the page of the Guest book of the Davyton House

"Gentlemen, please use the following page for your signatures. The space below the Governor General's signature is reserved."

"You have great expectations, Mr. Smikle," said McGuire.

"Yes, Mr. McGuire, expectation is that which lies in the hearts of all people. Time is the essence of its fulfillment. When a seed is sown, the expectation comes from divine mystery."

"Beautiful words," said McGuire.

"Can I offer you gentlemen some refreshment, perhaps tea?"

"Oh, it would be a pleasure," said Sergeant Buxton, "but we will be leaving in a few minutes in the interest of time."

"You seem to have done a lot of traveling, Mr. Smikle," commented McGuire.

"Well, I have been to Europe, the United States, and Canada. While living in England, I visited France and a few other countries."

"Would you consider giving me an interview at a later date, Mr. Smikle?" asked McGuire.

"What kind of interview do you have in mind, sir, may I ask?"

"Well, sir, I remember that you were here in Jamaica during the Christmas of 1988, distributing food and other items to the needy in this community who were suffering severely from the destruction of Hurricane Gilbert which, as you know, devastated the island in September of the same year."

"Oh yes, I remember receiving a letter from the Jamaican consulate in New York, extending a cordial thank you on behalf of the Government of Jamaica. Similar letters were also sent to three churches in New Jersey that responded promptly to my appeal for help. Jamaica Customs was also very helpful in their speedy clearance of the goods.

CONSULATE-GENERAL OF JAMAICA
TELEPHONE: 212 935-9000
CABLE: "JAMCONGEN", NEWYORK

866 SECOND AVENUE
NEW YORK, N.Y. 10017

OUR REF. NO. _____12/26_

November 21, 1989

Mr. Wilbert Smikle,
949 Ellis Parkway,
Edison
NEW JERSEY 08820.

Dear Mr. Smikle,

Thank you for your letter of November 14, 1989 regarding the three (3) churches that rendered such good service to us during our time of need.

I have written separately to the organizations concerned expressing thanks on behalf of the Government and people of Jamaica.

Many thanks for your kind intervention on this matter.

Yours truly,

Derick R. Heaven
Consul General.

The people who worked with me in the area should also be given credit, starting with the minister who gave me the list of the most needy. I never had the privilege of meeting any of the officials in the area, but I am sure many people had an enjoyable Christmas."

"Were you on the island during the hurricane?" asked McGuire.

"Very good question. I was right here in Davyton," I answered.

Sergeant Buxton interjected. "That was *really* a disaster. I was serving in Ocho Rios on the north coast resort area, and it was almost completely wiped out."

"I know, it was very hard to leave the island since the airports were closed," said McGuire apologetically. "We all had to wait. I made use of the time by helping to clean up the area."

"Mr. Smikle, I served on duty yesterday evening, and it is most pleasing that the Governor General offered you such esteem. Were you aware of the occasion prior to the event?"

"I was not. He knew of the service that is being rendered by this house and was asked to accept a bouquet of flowers, which would be given as he passed by. He preferred to enter the house as a matter of respect and was very gratified."

The three men rose from their seats. Sergeant Buxton expressed gratitude for my hospitality and promised to return for that cup of tea. McGuire appealed once more for an interview at a later date, and Corporal Brown remarked, "You surely have a beautiful home, Mr. Smikle." I shook their hands, escorted them to the gate, and waved a final goodbye.

Though their visit was not revealed to anyone, a small canary was somewhere around, quite unbeknownst to them.

Two weeks later, a friend of mine who is a justice of the peace with several degrees in gossiping, said to me, "Smikle, three officers paid you a visit. One is from the inspector's special branch of security. They drove in the inspector's car. What was the reason? I was hoping that you would mention the matter to me. First the Governor General visited you, and now, law enforcement. Only the custorlurium of the parish get such recognition. By the way, why didn't you offer them that good old rum instead of tea? Just joking. Believe me, that visit by his excellency was a fine gesture of esteem. You must be doing something good. Keep up the good work."

A Chance to Tell the Story

The result of that secret inquiry did not completely satisfy the authorities. Many questions remained. Detective Maguire was getting anxious and paid me a second visit.

In 1992, the wife of one of the dental group doctors asked if I would tell her the story of my life on her next visit. She never returned, but the idea remained. On Maguire's third visit, I informed him of my intention to write my autobiography.

Davyton Square.

Davyton is a small district situated in the rocky hills of central Manchester, approximately sixty miles from Kingston, the capital of the island. This area is part of the low mountain range that forms the backbone of Jamaica. Looking southeast in the far horizon is the beautiful Old Harbor Bay.

The eastern part of Davyton is bordered by a tall mountain range that blocks all views from beyond, except the rising sun or the lovely full moon. The nearest town is Mandeville, the capital of Manchester, which is seven miles south and in full view of Davyton. At night the lights in the town twinkle as they join the stars above in a constellation of galaxies. It's the island's most desirable resort area, with an average temperature of 60 to 88 degrees.

Balmy breezes from the blue Caribbean drift in from the south throughout the year. Some of the homes are of Elizabethan architecture; they are painted white with a taste of brown or gray trim, much to the desire of the middle and upper income families.

There is a small winding road that leads through Davyton. It branches from the main highway at Williamsfield and continues up the hills and gullies for four miles, where it rejoins the main thoroughfare at Mizpah. There, a small burial ground greets you with crosses and a ghostly aura. Tall trees seclude the homes along the roadway, and the shadows from the waving branches silhouette the mind when the moonlight breaks through the cloudy sky.

There are other side roads that lead to Davyton, where the large Congregational Church, which sits majestically on a small slope; the two-story Monumental Mission House, a symbol of Colonial days where the ministers reside; and also a community center are located.

There is also a field where cricket and football are regularly scheduled. The area is beautifully landscaped with roses, hibiscus, and other tropical shrubberies. Each year on Queen Victoria's birthday and other holidays special celebrations are held, and people with children from the neighborhood join in the merrymaking. The band plays and drums can be heard from many miles away.

My father was the first child of Robert and Rosa Smikle. He was born in 1880 at Richie Cumberland near the border of northeastern Manchester and Clarendon.

He married Ellen Carter from Babylon, Manchester, and moved to Davyton. He was six feet six inches tall, weighed 220 pounds and was very strong and fearless with a brilliant memory. Without glasses, which he seldom wore, reading was difficult.

He was gifted with a strong baritone voice and could sing most of the songs in the old Sankey. His voice could be heard from a far distance. As a revivalist preacher, he held prayer meetings on Sunday evenings at the local district square and in storefronts, much to the disapproval of the officers of the prestigious Davyton Church, of which he was a member. In spite of their differences, he was highly respected, as they remembered the occasions he had single-handedly broken up many fights, some unprovoked, and taken away their machetes.

Mother and Father Smikle

I was born on November 7, 1919, the third of nine children born of the wedlock in a small house which my father built on a rocky slope overlooking a gully, the bottom of which formed the base of a mountain range which rises over eight thousand feet.

There were six homes on small irregular lots of one to three acres owned by my neighbors. The path leading to these homes were small foot tracks, which became riverlets during the rainy season. The area is called Manny Hill, but in spite of the beautiful flowers and shrubberies, it was nicknamed the "Pissing Hole." Nicknames were also given to most of the people. They called my father "Joe Dog," and would refer to us as "Bra dog" or "pickinies."

Illustrative drawing of the "old homestead"

Many days while passing through the small village square with my father and other siblings, the jokers would start to bark and growl at us, much to our humiliation. Most of those who were jeering had their own nicknames: Bull Pus, Man Rat, Sly Mongoose, Man Simple, Chigger Foot. There was a small, highly respected man whom they called "Good Hood." He stammered, but the women didn't complain.

If you were sent to prison, you would be called "Prison Bird." There were many fights, and some people ended up in the hospital and the courts as a result of the calling of these nicknames, especially when they referred to women. The armed knights with their machetes were always ready to protect their lovers.

Our homestead of two acres was stony and tedious to work, but we had a small farm of potatoes, peas, corn, and coco as catch crops, and banana, coffee, mango, pimento, coconut, and oranges as perennials. We also raised chickens, goats, pigs, two dogs (Jack and Jim), and an old mule named Maggie.

My home was a small three-bedroom house with a sitting room. The floor, made of mortar, was kept polished with a red dye, and the sides were constructed of wackle and mortar. Every time a new sibling arrived, my father would quickly add a small room, like a honeycomb cell, to the main structure. As soon as I was old enough, I had to carry building materials of stones and wood from a nearby mountaintop. With the help of a one-armed carpenter, we joined one small room to another.

The kitchen was a small building very near to the main house. It had a three-legged pot hanging over the flame by a chain strongly secured to the ceiling. Around the flame was a circular wall about twelve inches high made of mortar with holes around the side. Those holes allowed air to feed the flame while the wall protected the fire from getting out of control. Our bathroom was adjoined to the main house; it always gave off a Detol scent with a hint of Lysol. Water had to be stored in a barrel at all times. The toilet was about one hundred feet south, and the wind blew from north to south, sending the carbon monoxide into the garden and trees, away from the house. It was the only structure inspected by the government's sanitation inspector, who would issue a summons to attend court if violations were found.

When hurricanes swept the island, all the zinc and boards that were not properly nailed down would dislodge and end up down in the gully. After retrieving them, my father would be back to the drawing board, patching up the areas and telling us of God's handiwork. The job showed no signs of professionalism, but with two coats of white wash and hibiscus, roses, and other flowers around, it created a scene of bewilderment and admiration.

Working from dawn to dusk, he acquired two more farms, one seven miles away in the flatlands of Cabbage Hall. During my school days, I spent a lot of time helping my father on the farm there. It was very fertile, watered by the constant flow from a nearby cave. Yams, potatoes, coco, and bananas thrived. Cabbage Hall got its name from the large cabbages it produces. My father would leave for Cabbage Hall on Monday morning, riding old Maggie on the main road, and return on Friday evenings with food supplies, which would be finished in three days. On Wednesdays, mother usually sent my younger brother David and I to Cabbage Hall for fresh supplies.

My older brother John and one of my elder sisters sometimes shared those trips to Cabbage Hall, but David was my companion on most of the voyages, whether getting firewood, food from the farms, or water from the reservoir at Bellefield, which was two miles away. David stammers and was quiet most of the time. When provoked, the words he uttered would be costly if heard by a policeman. In court a judge would issue a fine of one guinea or a jail term of thirty days.

The footpaths through the mountain to Cabbage Hall were treacherous and stony, with low hanging branches along steep cliffs in some areas. Every step of the way had to be carefully placed. We started out very early in the morning, through rain or sunshine, singing as we traveled along. Often frightened by the sudden outburst of a wild cat or sleepy owl, we went through a mile of muddy swamp, after which we climbed the last clustered slope. There, Jack and Jim would be waiting with wagging tails and growls to escort us to Cabbage Hall, which was a mile further away. The entire distance took three hours.

My father would welcome us with mint tea, sweetened by the juice of sugar cane, and roast yam or potatoes with a small piece of Codfish roasted on charcoal. We would quickly clean the area and load the barrels with water while he prepared our baskets with food. Jack and Jim escorted us to the usual spot, wagging their tails as if wishing they could follow us home, but we preferred not to leave our father alone in dismal, lonely Cabbage Hall.

With loads on our heads, it was silence all the way home. We had to walk carefully to avoid falls, which caused delays when the food was scattered and had to be retrieved.

Illustrative drawing of my brother David and myself

By the time we reached home, our clothes would be soaked with sweat or rain, the smell of which sent us straight to the wash house. It was always a joy for mother and my sisters to welcome us back home.

I attended Bellefield Elementary School, which was two miles from home. There was a narrow property which divided our small road from the main road. A bypass through that property to the main road saved us three-quarters of a mile when we were able to use it.

One of the neighbors had several dogs that hated children. Those dogs sometimes awaited us with the hope of getting a few bites. On several occasions, when just within a few yards of entering the main road, we were chased back to the point of entry. To prevent my younger siblings and other children with us from being bitten, David and I had to use all the stones and sticks we could find to throw at the dogs in order to slow them down. I was the leader and felt satisfied when we passed through the narrow bypass safely. When things went wrong, all the blame fell on me, even though at times we suffered bites. By the time we reached school, the teacher would be ready with his strap to render corporal punishment. He seldom punished the younger children, but we had to hold out the palms of our hands. And when he missed, he would make sure to land the punishment on our rumps.

Lunch time at school was always from 12-1 PM. Mother fixed lunch for the smaller children to take to school, but David and I had to return home for our lunch. A hot lunch called for speeding home. On cloudy days, when there was a lot of laundry, mother would be late reaching home, and we had to get the fire started to warm up the leftovers from last evening's dinner. There were flour dumplings, yams, and potatoes, mixed with small pieces of salt fish, cooked with coconut oil callaloo, scallions, and peppers. After drinking a large jug of limeade, it was difficult racing back to school with a heavy stomach. The sloshing noise sounded like a roaring river.

My teacher's name was John Thos. Hemans. He was a strict disciplinarian and had the habit of licking his tongue. The girls called him "Touch." Many of his students became scholars, educators, nurses, and civil servants. The founder of Clarendon College, the Rev. Lester Davy, was one of his graduates. He also helped me to pass my first year pupil-teacher examination with honors. The district people praised my parents for my achievements; some teased my father saying, "Bra dog family is moving up."

John Thomas Hemans

During those early years in elementary school, a few high schools on the island were located in Kingston, the capital. Only a few families could afford to send their children to those schools.

At Bellefield, children were encouraged to study for the first, second, and third year pupil-teacher examinations. Passing those exams brought prestige and respect to the child and his family. There were jealousies and suspicions when one child passed the exams and their neighbor's child failed. The neighbor whose child failed would end up at some obeah man, sixty or more miles away in a mountain hideout, trying to find out the reason their neighbor's child had succeeded. They would steal clothes of their neighbor's children (panties or a blouse, a boy's shirt or pants) when they were left to dry on the line in the backyard. They would pay the obeah man to make their child pass those exams and to "set goozou" on the neighbor to stop their children from being successful. My parents prayed for us night and day, even though my father was very good at seeing ghosts, but as I walked and worked with him, I was not able to see their shadows.

A teacher told my parents that John, my elder brother, showed great potential in learning. That is the compliment most families like to hear about their children. John was allowed more time in school and less time on the farm. After graduation from elementary school, he refused to study for the pupil-teacher examinations. My father anchored him on the farm, but not for very long. He started his own farm and had very little time to help my father.

Our lessons in school were explained on the good old blackboard. I had to take notes and borrow books from friends. The only other source was the public library, which was seven miles away in Mandeville, and they seldom had the books needed.

There were several girls in my class who were good looking, as we would say. They were great teasers and a lot of fun to be around. I learned a lot about women by listening to their gossip. All concentration on my studies came to an end when they started. Sometimes they would chase us away and call us "bwaay" whenever we abused our respect for them with a stare or a wink of the eye. They also threatened to report us to the head teacher, who would use a strap to make sure that we stayed under control. Those girls bragged about Sweet Sugar Brown, especially when they were in our company. Three or more would boast "he is my sugar," and another would say, "Oh no, no." Then other girls would join in the Sweet Sugar contest, which really made us jealous.

Brown was a tall, handsome, light-complexioned young man with straight black hair. He was a truck driver who did not know of the girls' infatuation with him. They only glanced at him occasionally when he drove through the area. I tried to win their affection but couldn't find a way to appeal to them. They all wanted "Sugar." When they passed by, I could hear them whispering, "Oh, Sweet Sugar." Many of them went on to gain professional recognition in the academics and nursing fields.

My mother depended on me to do errands. She sometimes complained that there was no money. She waited until the pot was on the fire before sending me to buy mackerel or other groceries from the Chinese man's grocery store in Bellefield. The smallest coin was a farthing, which is half of one cent. She sometimes gave me a quatty, two pence, or four bits. The Chinese store owner would make sure that a farthing, though small, was left with him, even if he had to sell me a grain of salt. I could "clip" the four-mile round trip before the water in the pot started to boil, sometimes losing a toenail when skipping across the sharp stones on the roadway. That toe would be sore and prevent the wearing of shoes on Sundays.

I never complained of being hungry. There were many trees with all kinds of fruits and nuts, some sweet, others sour. The plums seemed to have little worms inside the prettiest ones, but once in my mouth, down the gullet they went. In rainy seasons our clothes would be soaked. Mother had to wash them, then use the hot iron to dry and prepare them for us to wear to school daily. Most of our clothes were bought from the sale of eggs, surplus food, goats, or pigs.

My sisters were stubborn, but mother pressured them to help her. I kept her supplied with whips from the bassider tree. Those whips, nice and slender, didn't break easily and surely could sting. She would wait until night when they were assembled for bed. The crying and hollering would wake up the roosters and dogs around the neighborhood, causing some neighbors to grumble and complain. My father would be seven miles away at Cabbage Hall, snoring under the musical serenade of toads and crickets. The next day everything would be quiet, but the girls would give me a sad face, some sticking their tongues while others "cut their eyes."

In surrounding districts and towns, the police and other blacks showed great admiration for the whites in the area. Whites owned thousands of acres of land, which they had fenced or walled in to keep intruders out. The district people referred to them as "Backra." They would sometimes hunt wild hogs on horseback with their friends. To protect their properties, they hired blacks to watch their estates. They gave them uniforms with safari helmets and horses to patrol on. Black people called them "Busha," and because of their loyalty to their masters and their disregard to their own people, they were thought to be "stooges". Many people went to jail for stealing firewood or fruits. Wild hogs could not be stolen because of the noise they made. Backras owned estates all over the island, occupying the best agricultural land. Black farmers had to travel to the mountainsides or a valley far from home to plant crops. As a small boy, I thought white folks were angels with wings hidden under their clothes. Everyone seemed so white and clean looking, like pictures I'd seen in the Bible and other books. I thought they never took baths. All the women seemed to love white men. People believed that being favored by whites brought prestige to their families.

I was a member of Davyton Congregational Church and a Sunday school scholar. The Missionary Society in England built the church in 1843. It is located only one-third of a mile from my home. Its large bell could be heard from miles away. All ministers were white men from Britain. They would read most of their sermons, with an accent barely understood, but the members loved them and would travel many miles on foot or rode a donkey in order to be on time. Buses and taxies were scarce. Black ministers very seldom preached because the members didn't want to hear them.

On one occasion, a minister returned to England for a short time and a black minister by the name of Atkinson was chosen to serve in the interim. The officers and members quarreled and created hardship and havoc. Although Parson Atkinson was a brilliant Jamaican preacher, some felt the church had lost its prestige. The bitterness continued until the white minister returned. It was important to be a member of the Davyton Congregational Church since most jobs or schools of higher education required a recommendation from the minister, or Justice of the Peace, in order to be accepted.

The Salvation Army was the only other recognized group, though revivalists were scattered all over the island.

My mother prayed for our safety night and day. She never said an unkind word. As the number of sisters and brothers increased, I learned to accept responsibility, but failed in controlling their eating habits. When we ate locusts and rose apples, mixed with plums and mangoes, followed by a bowl of red pea soup, our stomachs would be swollen with colic and the belching and hollering would annoy my mother. She would quickly concoct an antidote by boiling different bush herbs for us to drink. Vomiting would be induced and we would be well again. She'd then give us a cup of mint tea mixed with ginger to complete the treatment.

The first white man to visit our home at Manny Hill was the minister of the Davyton Congregational Church, the Rev. Walter L. Lewis. He wore a white, short-sleeved shirt and white pants with crepe-soled shoes, which we called "pus" because of the soft rubber soles, which were very comfortable on the stony road.

Our dogs caught his unusual scent from a distance and went after him with no respect. He seemed to show no fear, and the dogs just stopped in front of him and flicked their tongues and growled. They never attempted to take a bite as they would with other people.

John, my eldest brother, was away, so David placed a small rope on each of the dogs and led them away. The other children scrambled towards the kitchen, where they sat on a bench and peeked through the spaces between the old boarded wall. My father and mother welcomed the minister and placed a chair under the small guango tree for him to sit in because the breeze was so refreshing. He spoke with an accent, which was Welsh. My mother kept smiling and nodding her head while Pa made excuses for not attending church services more often. He quoted verses from the Bible, and the minister seemed surprised that he knew so much, and praised him. We were called to meet the minister, who was no stranger to me since I had seen him many times at church services. I came out, bowed slightly and said, "Good morning, sir." All the other children followed suit and then returned to the kitchen.

He complimented the beautiful dahlias and roses, and mother was pleased that the area was clean from the constant sweeping. He expressed delight in meeting the family and wanted to know how my parents were making out with so many children. My father said, "It no easy at all, Sa," and offered him white yam, which is the most delicious of all yams. He accepted and asked that they be delivered to the mission. He then shook my parents' hands and said goodbye and that he hoped to see them again.

My father escorted him to the gate and watched as he climbed the stony hill, then waved as he went out of sight. It was jubilation after he left, the tense moment was eased, and everyone started to laugh and talk. The girls remarked about his wavy hair, long pointed nose, and small mouth.

The news of his visit spread all over the district and reached Mandeville, seven miles away. At school the girls warned me not to get fresh or allow the visit to go to my head.

I took part in a Sunday school concert. The teacher gave me a poem to learn entitled "I Would Like to Be a Gentleman." It was long with several humorous verses. I wore a formal black and white suit made from paper, shiny black patent leather shoes, a top hat and gloves, and carried a small cane, as many English gentlemen do. With the crowd staring, many children forgot their parts. Later I was called to perform my part. There was no curtain; you had to step from the door of an adjoining room onto the stage. With hat in hand and waving my cane, I performed a few dance steps. I recited my poem, "I Would Like To Be A Gentleman":

> *"...the kind of man with power to command and servants to obey my orders, the kind of man with dignity that commands respect, and gain the love of beautiful ladies, that I Want you all to know."*

I tipped my hat and waved my cane with assurance. The crowd applauded loudly. Then with a serious nod, I bowed graciously and left the stage, but the applause continued. Suddenly I reappeared and bowed a second time, saying, "And that I want you all to know, a man I'm sure to be. Count on me! I say, count on me."

After the affair was over, most of the "local upper crust" wanted to know who was that boy who recited the poem "I Would Like to Be a Gentleman?"

"That was Joseph Smikle's son," someone answered. "O yes, Bra Dog's son." From that day everywhere I went I was called "Mon."

There were three other farmers who had crops in the fertile area of Cabbage Hall. They had their own huts, but at nights they would assemble at David Williams' hut, which was the largest. He always had some rum to sell, which they would buy to cheer their spirits while playing dominoes and other games. Oh the tales they would tell of the many battles they'd fought against ghosts—commonly called "Duppies"—the hearts of the many lovers they'd broken, and how they'd outsmarted strict parents in order to seduce their daughters,

each trying to top the others with bigger and more outrageous lies. Some nights my father joined the group, but most times he stayed alone in his hut and meditated in the darkness, repeating verses from the Bible and listening to the sounds of various creatures of the night.

Whenever he was with the group, he'd buy a drink of rum, pour a handful on his head and neck, then rub those areas. The rest he would sip slowly. He liked to bring the scripture into the discussion. Some of these men knew the Bible very well and asked all kinds of questions, but they disliked the length of time he took to explain the answers. Sometimes they wished that he wasn't around, as they missed playing their games.

On one of our visits to Cabbage Hall, David and I were met by a big commotion. My father had prepared a piece of land in the valley near a dried up pond. One of the other farmers wanted that area and there was a quarrel that could not be resolved. The government owned the entire area of Cabbage Hall and the surrounding land, and they called it crown land, which meant that it belonged to the king. In those days, to speak against the king was treason against the crown, and you could be hung.

They sent for the overseer, who was a large brown man. He came dressed in a shinning khaki uniform and a large safari helmet. His horse was well groomed and the saddle was adorned with silver and chrome buttons. In addition, he wore a large belt around his waist with a large crown buckle, which clearly identified the head of the lion as a symbol of authority and strength.

He seemed to know the farmer who wanted the property, and arbitrarily told my father to choose another area. My father was very angry, but kept his temper and explained that the area was given to him by the previous overseer, but to no avail. He refused to listen. My father chose an area nearby a slope, and the other farmers helped him to prepare the new sight. It was customary for farmers to take turns and work in groups on each other's farm.

Down in the valley, the other farmer's crops were a beautiful sight. All looked forward to a great harvest. Before the plants started to produce food, it rained for seven days. All those lowland crops were destroyed. My father's farm on the hillside was safe from the flood rain and produced a bountiful harvest. That attractive flat land was ignored from that season, and no one tried to plant any crops there. My father gained respect as the stories spread of the flood of Cabbage Hall. He made sure that all the farmers who suffered the loss of their crops received a share of his bounty.

My father, being a revivalist preacher, would use a lantern and a drum, which he made from goatskin, to conduct meetings on Sunday evenings at the local square in our small district. I read the Bible for him and also supported mother and two of my older sisters by singing and clapping my hands while my brother John banged away on the drums. In the silence of the evening, our voices could be heard several miles away across the mountain. Many of the folks who could not afford the fancy clothes worn when attending the prestigious Davyton Congregational Church would join my father and receive great satisfaction from the meetings. They believed in his sincerity and kindness. Where other preachers would not visit the sick, especially those who lived in areas where the paths were difficult to travel, my father would.

There were many nights when he had to close the meeting in a hurry. In the silence of prayer, bad boys in the darkness not far away would growl and bark like dogs. Next, a hail of stones would land near the crowd. The police would sometimes investigate, but no arrests were ever made. This did not discourage my father, who made sure to secure his own surveillance. Many officers of the Davyton Congregational Church welcomed the disturbances because they didn't like those meetings, which were sometimes loud and lasted late into the night.

There was a revivalist preacher from Alston, a small district six miles from Davyton, whose name was Brother Facey. He came to Chantily, the adjoining district, with his wife, two daughters, and two other members of his church. The first night he preached in the open air, several people were converted, including some members of the Davyton Congregational Church. The news of his preaching spread rapidly, and my parents, after several attendances, were also converted to this new denomination.

They were completely changed and spoke in tongues, languages I could not understand. They were praising the Lord and saying Hallelujah, night and day. Within three months, they built a large thatched building in an open field belonging to one of the new converts. The seats were rough, wooden planks that were cushioned by pillows. Some of the bad boys whom they called hooligans, tried to break up the meetings, but to no avail. In fact, many of them were also converted and joined the church.

The large congregational church lost many of its members, and they were against this new intrusion. They scorned Brother Facey and tried to discourage the spreading of the new ministry, but evangelism had found its place under the dynamic preaching of this new leader. Some of the meetings lasted until very late, and my parents found it difficult to perform their farming duties.

My father gave up farming at Cabbage Hall and rented a piece of land from Busha Heron in nearby Shooter's Hill, three miles from home. The land was not as fertile, but he was happy to give more time to the work of the Lord.

A new church was built within three years. It was called The Chantily New Testament Church of God. My parents, who were charter members, helped to lay the cornerstone.

I was a lover of music and seldom missed school dances. Jim, a classmate who had learned to dance while living in Kingston, showed me a few steps. While the adults were in the dancing area, their daughters were in an adjoining room chaperoned by pupil-teachers. We were allowed in this adjoining room, where the music was loud enough for us to enjoy dancing. The lamps were dim, and that made those occasions very much to our satisfaction, and also those of the teachers, usually a couple, who would be out of sight most of the time.

Whenever there were gatherings or family members returning from abroad, there would be dancing and merrymaking. Jim and I would be the uninvited guests watching the older folks dance the quadrille, rumba, fox trot, or waltz. The men were dressed in white shirts and black or colorful pants; the women wore colorful, wide-pleated, long dresses with trimming all over. Their turban headwear reflected scenes from African celebrations. The drinks were rum punch or strong back, which is made from various roots and vines. Just the smell puts your feet in a dancing mood. There was always plenty of food to eat: rice and peas with curry goat, jerk pork, and chicken flavored with hot spicy sauce.

The nights were sometimes very dark when we returned home from the dances. The moon would sneak in and out of the clouds, and the shadows drove fear into my heart as I remembered those moments at Cabbage Hall and the tales the men told of ghosts and evil spirits.

Yet, night after night I seldom heeded the pleas of my father to keep away from those dances. Most nights I had to be home before 1:00 AM so as not to disturb my mother. In the morning, I was the first to rise, making sure to keep away from Pa, who believed in not sparing the rod. My mother would threaten me without disclosing my absences to Pa.

In school my favorite subjects were history, geography, arithmetic, and the scripture. Under colonial powers, we were taught that England was our mother country. I had always believed that my parents originated from Africa, but many of the stories heard from that country were barbaric. We had to know about every ruler of England, their birth, their deeds and acts, battles won, and their many lords and dukes. *How can there be so many lords?* I always wondered, since the scripture says there is only one Lord, the Lord above.

In Jamaican history, we had to know the names of every Governor since the island was captured from Spain three hundred or more years before, and also the names of all the great English men of valor and honor: Walter Raleigh, Admiral Penn, and they even mentioned and honored Henry Morgan, the pirate. Most of the parishes were named after kings, governors, saints, and dukes. The heads of government were always whites sent from Britain—the governor, police commissioner, director of education, most of the judges, the head of civil servant, and the regiment. The local police forces were made up of blacks who were very strong and husky, though some were ignorant and ruthless. They had to keep their badges shined so that the crown could be seen on their uniforms at all times.

After graduation from elementary school, the teacher asked my parents to allow me to study for the Pupil-Teacher Exams. Being encouraged by my mother, father allowed me to leave at 2:30 in the evenings and prepare for the 4:30 to 6:30 PM classes. Without a clock, I had to listen for the Kingston to Montego Bay passenger train, which blew its whistle at 2:00 PM every day at the Williamsfield Crossing. At night I studied, keeping the kerosene lamp burning until the oil ran out. Whenever I missed a day from the farm, my father complained and repeated the same old stories about how two bulls can't reign in the same pen and that children must obey their parents in the name of the Lord.

I failed the first year exam, much to the disappointment of my parents. My friend Jim was successful and moved up to the second year. I had to take the first year over and was humiliated sitting with the younger students.

The second time I passed the exam with honors. I was the only one in the class to gain that distinction, which certainly elevated my prestige. I now had to dress more respectably, so I took a day or two from the farm and worked at the United Fruit Company Citrus farm, weeding the high grass around the trees with a man whom the overseer knew. I earned money to buy some clothes and an extra pair of shoes. No one knew my identity, that I was 'The Man.'

Pupil-teacher examinations were getting tougher every year. Teacher colleges were accepting fewer scholars. The government started a practical training center for boys at Christiana Manchester, seven miles from my home. It was called Holmwood. The main subjects were agriculture, followed by woodwork and machinery.

In 1939 I applied for admission to Holmwood and was told to submit a recommendation. I went to the Justice of the Peace, Mr. D. D. Philips, who was a deacon at Davyton church and a very prominent agriculturalist. He was reluctant, remembering that my parents were worshiping with Brother Facey. His daughter reminded him that I was 'The Man.'

"Which Man?" he asked

"That young fellow who recited that poem."

He asked me to recite the poem once more. After hearing it, he inquired if my father could support me at the new school. I assured him that the training was free and I would be a day student. He was satisfied and asked his daughter to type a recommendation for me. When handing it to me he said, "Now my boy, I want you to be a man, and don't let me down." I gratefully thanked them both and hurried home.

The following day I walked seven miles and delivered the sealed letter to the secretary of Holmwood Practical Training Center. The superintendent, E. B. Roger, told me that they were accepting only ten students for the class of 1939, and a special examination would be held to select ten students from sixty applicants. On my way home, the sound of "You little tiny grub!" was heard coming from two seniors nearby. First year students at Holmwood were called "grubs," no matter what size you were. A grub is a tiny, slippery substance that must be seen and not heard. He must obey all seniors at all times, with respect and honor.

My observation of the school gave me the assurance that somehow there were things to gain. Those young boys in their nice khaki uniforms, pruning citrus trees on a nearby farm, seemed to be enjoying their work. There was noise coming from a play field, where a game of football was in progress, and that gave me a feeling of satisfaction. The sweet smell of food from the kitchen stirred my hunger, but then I had to hurry because home was seven miles away.

One month later, I was notified by an official letter O.H.M.S. (On His Majesty's Service). I was instructed to present myself for a special examination at the Holmwood Practical Training Center for Boys. It also carried a note informing me that the ten students securing the highest marks would be selected. The day of the examination, I was surprised to see so many large boys, some weighing more than one hundred and fifty pounds. We were told that the successful students would be notified by mail. The Post Mistress was getting tired of my presence, as anxiety took over as I awaited a response.

On the fourth week I received another "O.H.M.S." letter, which instructed me to return to Holmwood for the process of elimination because nineteen boys had achieved the highest marks. On that day, a physical examination reduced the number to fifteen students. I was weighed for the first time, and the doctor told me that my weight was ninety-eight pounds and my height was five feet three inches tall. I was among the fifteen boys from which ten students would be chosen.

They selected four third-year students to take us to two different citrus farms. Two senior students received eight boys, and the other two received seven boys. On the farm they gave us each a machete to weed the high grass from around the tender citrus trees. Some of the eight boys in my group were resentful. Without a word, I started to do the job. Others did the same, but grumbled as they did. After an hour, we were all asked to assemble in the dining room, where a nice lunch was served. We were instructed to return home until further notice. No one asked my age and I never revealed it, but I was twenty years old, while many of the larger boys were only sixteen to eighteen years of age. Two weeks later, I received a special letter, which I opened as quickly as possible. It was a joy to read the large print which said, "Congratulations and Welcome to the class of 1939 Holmwood Practical Training Center."

My first semester began in September of 1939. I left home after the first cock crows, which was about four or four thirty, and reached school at seven thirty in the morning. The government gave us breakfast at 8 AM and lunch at 12 noon. They also gave us two khaki suits each year.

Illustrative drawing of the "old homestead" at night.

Our superintendent was a very religious man who led us in devotion and lectures every morning from 8:30-9:00, ending with our favorite song, "Now Thank We All Our God." We spent at least three days per week on the farm and the other two days in workshops. Lectures were given on the job by junior masters and instructors. Agriculture and animal husbandry were the main subjects, followed by woodworking, mechanics, and iron working.

Those who excelled in agriculture were given a special scholarship to the Government Farm School. B.H. Easter, the Director of Education, and the school superintendent were very close friends. Some fellows who lived very close to the school received special training from one of the staff, a brilliant teacher. He would teach them after 4 PM, and they would pass the third year Pupil-Teacher examination with honors, after which they would have to seek additional education elsewhere. One of them became the superintendent of a practical training center; another, a prominent attorney.

Parents who objected to the hazing of their sons were told that "boys will be boys," and that the motto of the school, FACTA NON VERBA, was to promote men who would be strong and respected in deeds, not words. Due to my size, senior men did not bother me too much, but on many occasions they gave me a punch or two for good measure. One day I was asked by one of the senior men to repeat the Grub rules, to which I quickly responded. Then I was asked to repeat the rules a second time. When asked a third time, I hesitated and was immediately greeted with a hard punch to the face. With all those seniors looking on, I lifted the gentleman into the air and threw him on the hard gravel. Before I could pin him down, a few seniors jumped me and dragged me to the showers, where they drenched my new khaki uniforms and then added a few bruises. Some of the third year students who saw the incident were embarrassed that it had taken four seniors to subdue me, the tiny grub. They didn't know my age, that I was indeed a man, and a very strong one. I was very seldom attacked physically, but in the dining room the food came to me late and there was very little left.

"A small Grub can't eat too much," they would say. On the farm I was asked to wash all the tools, even though many of my first-year classmates were standing by. "A strong Grub don't need any help," they would say.

There was a ditch very close to the woodworking area where sawdust and wood shavings were dumped, where Grubs had to leap 15 to 20 feet down when they were being chased by the seniors to avoid harassment. I refused to take those leaps and would end up getting punished.

I walked to Holmwood for the first six months, leaving home very early in the morning. We didn't have a clock, so we had to depend on the moon or the crowing of roosters. My mother was very good at determining the time for me to wake up, even though she went to bed very late at night.

When I missed breakfast at 8 AM I had to wait for lunch. If I had a penny I would buy a bulla, which is a small bun that had to be shared with the seniors. The road to school was rough and very hard on my feet, so I had to take my shoes off and walk barefoot until I reached within a half mile from school. Then I would put them on.

Along the seven miles was a narrow section with many deep corners and low hanging trees overshadowing the roadway. In that area is the Mizpah cemetery. People were afraid to walk that dismal road at night. They talked of seeing ghosts as they walked into those shadows, and they sometimes fainted. Whenever there were new graves, the air around would be filled with Khus Khus, a high perfume some of the families used to reduce the morbid smell. I never saw any shadows of ghosts during those early mornings.

Early one morning when I left for Holmwood, the moon was hidden beyond the clouds, but all seemed well as I trotted along the lonely road. Somehow I felt sleepy, but the gentle breeze kept me awake. As I approached a dark corner, the clock at the Mizpah Methodist Church struck 4 AM. Suddenly a large shadow appeared several feet in front of me, waving as if warning me to stop. As the breeze increased and the trees swayed I waited, eyes searching to see the direction from where the shadow had come. I moved a few steps forward and just then the shadow appeared a second time. Fear and confusion caused my feet to shake and my tongue to swell. At 4 AM my heart told me to take heed and turn back. I was now convinced that the fabled ghost was really roaming the area. Moments later the moon came out of the cloud and a gentle breeze swayed the branches of a large tree, revealing the shadow that slowly floated across the road. It was so real, and the swaying of the trees coincided with the waving shadow. There was no one sitting on the wall and no fragrances as I moved forward.

There were no buses or taxis for transportation, and very few people had cars. Walking was the only way to get to Holmwood. Students who lived more than five miles were each given a bicycle after six months of walking. The superintendent had never met my parents, but was very encouraging. Knowing the distance I had to walk every day, he made sure I was given a bicycle by the government. The first evening I rode home with my brand new shining bicycle, all the boys in the district wanted a spin. Very few could ride, but they would assemble at the good old Look Out Pen Common and receive a few minutes of practice on the smooth cricket field.

To avoid them, I started to spend extra time in the cabinet working shop at Holmwood making small picture frames, hat racks, and small tables from scraps of wood, which I would join and clamp together. Those small projects earned me a few shillings.

After riding the bicycle for about a year, my weight increased to one hundred and thirty pounds and my height to five feet seven inches, so in my second year I started to exercise my seniority to the new first year "grubs." My second and third year peers showed a lot of respect for me, especially on the cricket field. I was a good batsman and teammate.

Rainy days gave me more time in the workshop where building furniture, doors, and windows were made under the strict supervision of Father Bailey, an old man who was an expert cabinet maker. We called him "Poopa" because he would always break wind, and we dared not laugh. I did a lot of sanding and polishing, along with jointing and repairing broken furniture for some of the supporters of the school who served on the school board.

One of my peers, named Kerr, was a genius in the workshop. So good was he at cabinet working that they gave him most of the intricate projects. Although he took a lot of abuse as a Grub by the seniors, we became friends and spent a lot of time together in the workshop. In the summer most of the resident students went away on holiday. A few fellows, including Kerr and I, would be paid a few shillings to work on furniture. Kerr loved to sing, and before lunch, when I was hungry, just listening to him would annoy me. I just couldn't figure why he never seemed to be hungry.

One day he sneaked away from the job at ten in the morning. My curiosity prompted me to spy on him. He went towards the back of the kitchen, which was partially secluded by shrubberies. The cook placed a large pot of pasteurized milk on the windowsill to be cooled by the breeze. The milk was brought from the farm. As I watched, he pulled a small plastic tube from his bosom and, though the window was almost closed, he pushed it through the cracked window and into the milk. He sucked a belly full, after which he slowly retracted the tube back into his bosom and zig-zagged his way back to the workshop. The cooks were busy elsewhere and no one saw him. The cream on top of the milk remained unbroken, and it was difficult to tell that some of the milk was missing. They thought that milk reduced while cooling. He returned to the workshop, and within minutes the air was filled with his favorite song, which was sung each morning, "Now Thank We all Our God." He had no idea his secret had been discovered.

The next day I started to look around for a tube similar to the one he had used. My search led me to the machine shop, where I found a sample of the tube. It was dirty, but I cut a portion long enough to do the job. I washed it thoroughly, and then I waited until the cooks were in the adjoining kitchen washing dishes and gossiping. The job was easier than I thought, and the result was rewarding. An hour later Kerr started his singing, and I joined him loud and clear. He gave me a startled look as if to say he didn't care for a duet. Things went well with me for quite some time as I continued to enjoy my new discovery.

One day while I was having my portion of milk, one of my peers, a third year student, caught me. His name was Morgan. He couldn't believe what he had seen and threatened to report me to the superintendent unless I gave him my tube so he could have his share. The first day after Morgan had his share, they moved the milk from that window and placed it somewhere else, and all our singing and joy came to an end.

There was an old lady living in Davyton whose name was Caroline.

Caroline Haynes

The district people called her "Cousin Carry" for short. We were related, but I wasn't sure how. My father told me that his grandfather was first cousin to her husband. People who were well off didn't want to hear of any distant relatives linking to their family, especially if they were at the bottom of the ladder financially. She lived alone in a large white house with a lattice front on the veranda. She liked flowers and had lovely roses all around her lawn. Most of her children lived in America and Canada, with the exception of a son who was the manager of a machine shop on a large sugarcane estate in Jamaica. She had a grandson in Kingston who attended Calabar High School, and he came home only on holidays. They sent her money regularly, and by selling coffee, pimento, oranges, and other produce from the large property, she was considered very rich by many, and highly respected, being the sister of the prestigious Justice of the Peace, D.D. Phillips, who had given me the letter of recommendation to attend Holmwood.

Since the foot path to my home in Manny Hill was narrow and had a lot of sharp stones sticking out of the ground, I asked Cousin Carry permission to leave my bicycle at her home where it could be safely locked away. Most evenings she would leave pepper pot soup for me, and my mouth would burn with the first taste.

One day she asked me to write a letter because she told me that whenever she tried, her hands would shake uncontrollably. I became her secretary and was the only person allowed in her house, other than the cleaning lady who worked two days per week. She would leave small amounts of money in different places around the house that I would find and give to her. Sometimes she would return them to me for being an honest boy.

Students were required to demonstrate the art of systematic farming by creating a small farm project at home. Cousin Caroline gave me a portion of land to make my farm projects. All my seeds were germinated on scaffold beds. I would place four or six posts in the ground, then lathe them off horizontally with small sticks, followed by grass for bedding, and cover the grass with fine top soil. The seeds would be safe from ants and bugs. My fertilizer was the droppings from bat caves mixed with a small portion of perforated lime. The tomatoes, cabbage, and eggplants were of tremendous size and my project was the most admirable in the area.

While in elementary school I received a few hours of music lessons from a retired schoolteacher, Mary Jane Morgan, but was unable to continue because of my busy schedule. One of Cousin Caroline's sons, by the name of Aston, paid a visit to Jamaica from the United States. He brought a large piano with him and left it in the living room. Cousin Caroline encouraged me to practice on the piano. She felt it would keep it in tune.

One day while I was practicing, her son from the sugarcane estate in Jamaica paid her a surprise visit. He demanded to know why I was in the house and playing the piano. Before she could give him an answer, he asked me to leave the premises. His mother took exception to the rude behavior of her son. He didn't know that his mother was unable to write and that I had been doing all her correspondence to him and all the other members of the family in strict confidentiality. When she told him, he apologized to me.

My parents, though respected, were not recognized by many of the district people as among the "who's who," and by joining the New Testament Church of God, they were ostracized. Not long after that incident, Gerald, the nephew of Cousin Caroline and the son of the Justice of the Peace who gave me the letter of recommendation, came to see me. He wanted to know everything about Holmwood Training Center. I did not know the reason for his inquiries, but a few months later her grandson, Howard Hall, joined me at Holmwood as a boarding student. He showed great interest in iron work and was allowed to pursue that course.

A third training center was opened in the western part of the country, and I was selected to teach students the basics of systematic agriculture for a short time. The Government acquired a large estate at Chudleigh, which is two miles from Holmwood, and divided it into five-acre plots for graduates who could afford the small initial cost of ten pounds. I could not afford it.

My 1941 graduation was highlighted with many long speeches by dignitaries and officials of the school. They told us to go out into the world and be men of value, to be proud and carry the name of Holmwood forward and be loyal subjects of our country.

For my graduation I was given agricultural equipment to start my own farm. I decided to put my experience to work by renting farmland in my district. I also continued my job in woodworking at Holmwood when the opportunity arose.

The Dreams

God works through his chosen, his purpose to fulfill. I was twenty-two years old when in a dream I found myself working on a rooftop with hundreds of other men doing similar work on other buildings. The area covered hundreds of acres, with the sea not far away. With hammer and nails, I pounded away, keeping pace with the men as we laid the roofing down. *Where could that place be in Jamaica?* I asked myself. *Oh no, this is just a dream.*

Not long after my first dream, a second dream came to me. I was one of six men who stood gazing at a large farm. A hundred or more acres of tender stems sprouted from the ground six to ten inches high with no leaves. *Where could that be, a farm so large; yet not of sugar cane?* Within days the matter was forgotten.

My third dream was the scene of a large city almost completely destroyed. Large buildings piled up in rubble, as far as I could see. There were churches with pinnacles on the ground and crosses broken in pieces among the bricks. Since there was no earthquake in Jamaica, that dream was just another dream, soon forgotten.

My fourth dream took place at Manny Hill, where I stood and saw a bright light traveling in the eastern sky from north to south. The noise it made was heard by one and all as it disappeared towards the capital of the island. Those twinkling lights were not stars, and planes that large had not been made in 1941.

In my fifth dream I was walking on the stony road towards my home one evening as the sun faded away in the twilight. Suddenly, the figure of a mother holding a child in her arms appeared in the eastern sky. A bright light around the head of the babe reminded me of pictures I had seen somewhere in books.

As I observed the scene, the eyes of the child focused on me, beckoning me to come.

The fulfillment of each dream brought words and music to my soul with a melody for each. My voice rang out in praise to God.

In the spring of 1942 I was employed by the school to work in the cabinetmaking department. After that assignment was completed, carpenters were needed by the US government to build barracks at Fort Simmons in Sandy Gully, a section of the southern coastline that has a good harbor for large ships. The superintendent immediately transferred several of us to do that very important job. It was the first major construction in the country and several hundred men were employed to begin work. My first pay was two pounds, eight shillings per week. More than fifty buildings, covering several hundred acres, were being constructed at the same time. While on top of one of those building, with hammer and nails in hand, I suddenly realized there were hundreds of men around me doing the same thing. This first dream of my youth was revealed, and right before mine eyes. The building top of Fort Simmons seen, with me in the midst—"An act of God came true."

The buildings of Fort Simmons, 1942.

The Dreams Of Youthful Days - Dream #1

Words and Music: Wilbert Smikle

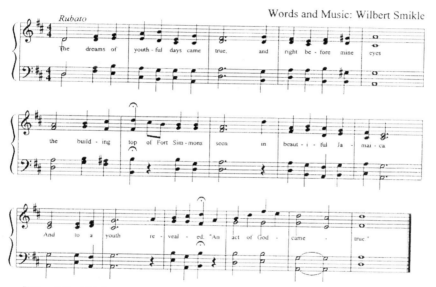

Dream of Youthful Days was sung when each came true, confirming 'An Act of God.'

I'll never forget the night I brought my first week's pay home and showed it to my mother. Not a check, but pure cash in a nice, small, brown envelope. How sweet it was. She returned a portion to me and told me to begin some dental work. "I want you to smile," she said gently.

Every morning I caught the train from Williamsfield Station to Fort Simmons. People in the district called me "Mr. Man." We worked overtime on many occasions and sometimes on Saturdays. With overtime, the pay was more than a dream.

News of job opportunities spread all over the island, and thousands of men and women flocked to the area seeking a piece of the pie. Most of the men were professionals and complained bitterly when told that the employment office was closed and that jobs would be available soon. They hung around hoping to be employed in any kind of job. Even the common laborers made three hundred percent more at Fort Simmons than elsewhere.

The Americans built tall fences with barbed wire around the compound and hired security guards to prevent any intruders from entering the restricted area. Only workers with badges were allowed through the gates. The vast area around the base was flat land, belonging to the government of Jamaica.

People came from Kingston, the capital, and all over the island and established residence. They built shacks, kitchens, and huts from boards, zinc, and other scrap materials, most of which were taken from the base. The roads to the compound were jammed with all kinds of traffic: old cars (some broken down), new vehicles, donkey carts, and large trucks carrying stones and other materials. Some people carried their families and animals with them; dogs, cats, goats, pigs, and cows were roaming all over. When it rained, the mud was intolerable. I was secure and so were many of my friends and co-workers. The good money coming from America was a surety. News circulated that the American Government had leased the area from England for ninety-nine years and that the jobs would last for a long, long time.

Some people began to expand onto their homes; they borrowed money from banks and other lending institutions, hoping that the good money would continue to flow. I never missed a day. Most of the Americans were old builders and engineers, some in military uniforms. They spoke with a southern twang. They would swear and threaten to fire anyone who moved slowly. They didn't care so much about neatness; they were more concerned about speed. If you drove a nail and it bent, you just threw it away and used a new one.

Earning sixteen to eighteen pounds for working overtime for one month was unbelievable. Many top government officials were making only five to ten pounds per month.

The job came to a sudden stop within nine months, and most of us were laid off permanently. Those who laid the foundation for big plans found themselves in debt and blamed the government for the ninety-nine-year lease that did not materialize.

I spent a few months working with my father to add a new room to the house and making improvements to the bathroom. The money I had earned was able to ease the financial burden. My father was able to hire more help, and my mother made sure that the girls were taken care of with outfits, which were a necessity.

Most of my front teeth had been taken out, and I was saving towards dentures when the lease came to an end. The girls teased me, asking me to smile, and when I opened my mouth, they would laugh and scatter off in all directions. Not long after, my dentures were ready, and when I smiled, they all smiled with me.

In early spring of 1943, I was one of several persons re-hired at Holmwood to work on a special assignment to build furniture while the regular students were on holiday. New furniture orders had been delayed, and I was anticipating a layoff.

Mr. Shelito was a friend of the superintendent. He served on the Board of Directors of Holmwood while I was a student, and had known me as the student who had repaired his broken antique furniture. He was selected by the government to recruit farm workers from the surrounding areas to work on farms in the United States. He was issued a number of cards to distribute to farm workers for them to receive a physical examination. Although it was kept a secret, I heard about it.

On my way from Holmwood, I stopped at his residence and asked for one of the cards. He told me quite frankly that I was not eligible, being that I was not a farm worker. I explained that I had three years of training at school as a farm worker. Though not convinced, he gave me a card with a warning not to tell anyone at Walderton while passing through that district. The physical examination was scheduled for the next day.

While on the job, the superintendent called some of the workers who were scheduled to be laid off to a special meeting. He informed us that the recruiting agent had not met the quota for farm workers at Christiana and that he would be willing to personally escort those of us who wanted to go to America to the physical agent, even though we had no cards. Within two hours ten of us successfully passed the physical examination.

There were several hundred men outside the center seeking the opportunity to take the test, but they had no cards. Among them was a friend from my district, Alfred. He was very happy for my success and regretted not having a card. I was hoping to give the card I'd received to my brother John, but he was away. I took Alfred to Mr. Shelito and informed him that I had passed the physical and would like for him to give my unused card to Alfred. He changed the names and submitted a letter to the agent explaining the reason. Alfred passed the test on the final day and we were scheduled to leave the island within two weeks.

My mother was worried because of what she'd heard about how blacks were being treated by whites in America. Having read about those large cities in America and England and observing visitors when they came to Jamaica, I was ready to take my chance.

There was a lot of talk about war efforts and what could be done to help our mother country, England, who was taking a pounding from the Germans. Ships were being torpedoed right near our island and fear of traveling on the ocean was in everyone's heart, but I needed money, and the United States needed my service. It was an opportunity beyond my imagination.

Alfred and I were the first to leave from Davyton as farm workers under the umbrella of the United States War Food Administration. On May 7, 1943, we left Jamaica, along with three thousand men, on board two U.S. transports. My ship had about two thousand men on board. There were several armed sailors on board to maintain order and discipline. After about six hours, the ship started to rock and dip as it rode the high seas. There was no land in sight, and I started to vomit, and it continued all night. The ship was a dreadful scene with sick men vomiting all over. For most of us, this was the first experience being on anything larger than a row boat.

It was dark on the water, and the men started to pray. To allay our fears, the sailors told us that two other ships would be escorting us from a convoy, and we would feel better as soon as we got something to eat. The next day we lined up for breakfast in circular rows. Round and round we went. The guards kept their eyes on us as the ship ploughed through the deep waters. The cooks could not keep up with the crowd and confusion started.

The men who had breakfast would get back in line for dinner, pushing those who were still waiting for breakfast. The guards started to shout and curse in their effort to maintain order. At the end of the second day, we were exhausted and unable to stand in line. Alfred fainted and four of us took him to the dispensary. The doctors ordered food and we all had a good meal. Other men started a fainting epidemic to try and bypass the long waiting lines. The doctor ordered the armed guards to disperse them and stop the congestion.

The ships were diverted into the Gulf of Mexico and docked at New Orleans, where we disembarked and were driven to an air force base. The trip took four days. While at the base, there wasn't much to see except those young pilots learning to fly, just barely missing our barracks while trying to get airborne.

On May 16, 1943, about seven hundred of us were placed on a freight train heading north. The train stopped at several small towns for coal, food, and water, which gave us a chance to refresh ourselves. I was thrilled to see so many long bridges over large areas of water. We were told that New Jersey was our destination. Finally, after two days, the train dropped us off at a camp three miles from the small town of Bridgeton in south Jersey.

My first picture on the farm.

A large number of shacks had been prepared for our lodging. Each shack had four beds with blankets folded neatly. In the center of each shack was a pot-belly stove with its funnel protruding through the roof. It was rather cold for us without sweaters or warm clothing.

None of us knew how to get the stove going, but it didn't take long for us to figure it out. The trouble was how to control that "red hot mama." One moment we would be hot, the next, cold again.

There was a large wooden building, which was divided into a mess hall, kitchen, coal storage bin, toilet, and bathroom facilities. Several nice chrome showers were inviting, but the water was ice cold, making all of us cough.

Alfred and Kerr were my close companions; we were always together. Kerr was a singer and dancer who was full of humor. Alfred was a lover boy, very smart with a quick temper and ready to fight for his rights.

Four days after we arrived, several farmers came to camp. I was one of six men, including Alfred and Kerr, assigned to work with a farmer three miles away from camp. I was shocked to see such a large farm, covering more than forty acres. It had rows of tender stems, twelve inches or more, sticking out of the ground with no leaves—*my second dream.*

Illustrative drawing of a field of Asparagus in south Jersey, 1943.

"These tender sprouts must be reaped," the farmer said. He gave us a small tool about thirty inches long with a double-edged tip, then showed us how to gently pluck the tender stems from the ground.

We lined each row with boxes. There was a man for each row, each ending eight hundred feet or more away. The farmer lit a small cigar, and with a tender voice he said, "See you boys at noon." Then he slowly drove away.

The constant bending caused severe pain of my back for the first two hours. The other fellows felt the same, but there was no way out. We slowed our pace, but that didn't ease the pain. Soon we stopped and rested and gazed from whence we'd started, and the many boxes we'd filled.

Not far away, the sound of many tractors was heard as other farmers quickly ploughed more land so that more crops could be planted before spring ended. Our thirsts went unquenched as we forgot to bring water with us. Out in the open field, the sun was extremely hot, and with no shade trees around, everyone just kept silent. At twelve we saw an approaching vehicle; the farmer was on his way with salami and corned beef sandwiches, along with sodas and a large drum of water. We helped him to load the filled boxes of asparagus on

The Dreams Of Youthful Days - Dream #2

Words and Music: Wilbert Smikle

Dream of Youthful Days was sung when each came true , confirming , ' An Act of God'.

the truck, and then he gave us a smile and said once more, "See you all at five, boys," and drove away. Some of the fellows didn't like being called "boy," but thought well of him in bringing us the food and water. In the open fields, we "went" in the bushes around us, but made sure to return as fast as we could, the tales of lions and tigers in the woods fresh on our minds.

After lunch, I looked at my watch, gave Alfred a nod, picked up my tool, and started to "pluck." Soon he was in his row. The other fellows soon joined in, and the plucking game was resumed with the same moaning and groaning. At five o'clock the farmer returned with a load of empty boxes, which we quickly replaced with filled boxes, then we piled in the back of the truck. He dropped us off at camp and then headed to the canning factory. We immediately went to the showers, but the cold water drove us away.

Not all men worked on the farm; a few were assigned to work in the kitchen preparing breakfast and dinner. The following evening, a meeting was held by the camp manager. Several concerns were discussed. The rate of pay was fifty cents per hour for forty to forty-eight hours per week. One dollar per day was taken out for meals, and one for savings. The savings were sent to Jamaica for us and given to us when we returned. All of our medical expenses would be the responsibility of the U.S. government.

All workers were to be ready to be picked up by their farmer no later than 7 AM. We were told to obey the laws of the country, to give Jamaica a good name, and to bear in mind that our presence on the farm was for the "war effort." We were also to remember our families back home in Jamaica.

Many of the farm workers in our group were of very fair complexion and considered to be white. They were from northern Manchester and St. Elizabeth and knew nothing about segregation or discrimination in Jamaica. They would not accept service at restaurants or bars unless their black Jamaican counterparts were served at the same time without prejudice.

The nearest town from camp was Bridgeton. To support the war effort under the War Food Administration, a special meeting was held by the town council. The people were told to put their feelings against the Jamaican farm workers on hold. The war must be won, the crops must be reaped, and everyone must make the supreme effort to cooperate and work together.

In spite of the appeal by the officials, some restaurants and bars were quite willing to serve the Jamaicans who looked like whites, but refused to serve blacks in the same group. Sometimes they all ended up in jail on a Saturday or Sunday night. On Monday morning, the police would hurriedly get them to camp to avoid confrontation with the WFA officials and the farmers whose crops couldn't wait.

I attended my first Sunday church service with Kerr, Alfred, and three other Jamaicans, one month after being at camp. Buses traveled from Philadelphia to Bridgeton regularly and passed very near to the camp. We caught the first bus that came along heading for Bridgeton. At the sight of the first church, we got off the bus and entered the large front doors of that beautiful church. The driver hesitated before moving on, but kept looking in our direction. I had no idea why, but was told later. The usher signaled an elderly white man, who whispered into his ears. They then showed us a row of seats in the rear. Alfred said, "We would be more comfortable nearer to the front, if you please." The usher then seated us in the center. Three whites moved out so that we all could sit together. There were no other blacks worshipping with them. The hymns were familiar and all of us raised our voices in harmony. We were the center of attention, and it felt good to be so admired by the congregation. The minister announced our presence and explained that we were from the West Indies and that our job in this country was to reap the crops since so many U.S. men had been drafted. He thanked us for our service and prayed that the war would be over soon so that everything could return to normal. Just before we left, two white men approached us and advised us that we would be more comfortable at our own church on the other side of town. I didn't know that all of us could have faced a jail for breaking the law, that June of 1943.

Our next visit to worship in Bridgeton took us to a Baptist church located on the other side of town, where most of the blacks lived. It didn't have the large high steps or beautiful front door like the first church, but they were adding a new section to accommodate a Sunday school. We felt the glory of the Lord as we were ushered in. The minister said, "Hallelujah; praise the Lord," and the people followed with a loud, "Amen." The minister spoke with a southern accent, delivering a long sermon. Some of the words I barely understood, but I knew the scripture and was able to follow his preaching. The blacks lived in a separate area of the town and many of them had heard of our visit to the white church but did not realize we were strangers in the country. As usual, the songs were familiar tunes and our voices could be heard as we joined in harmony. One of the ushers brought us to the attention of the congregation during the announcements. The minister welcomed us and asked for our names and a testimony. Our English, mixed with our Jamaican "patois," made it clear that we were strangers. We were given a formal welcome.

After service, food was served. We were introduced to southern fried chicken, collard greens, black-eyed peas, and corn bread. Many of the fellows reached for more and could have kept on all evening. To add to the delight, many young ladies focused their attentions on us, but more on the fair-complexioned men in our group. Some were invited to dinner the next time in town. I have always experienced problems with girls when in the company of fair-complexioned Jamaicans. Sometimes, it was in my best interest to avoid going places with them, so I clung to my close friends Alfred and Kerr.

I adopted the style of clothes worn by many of the young black men, like the zoot suit, as it was called. We found tailors who would make any style. The long, striped jacket, single or double breasted with wide lapels; the pleated pants with wide knees and a very small cuff above the pointed shoes; blended with a long gold chain hanging from the belt to the side pocket; capped by a very wide felt hat, with a wide brim. I thought with a little gold in my teeth, my smile would swing any beautiful girl into my waiting arms, but I had Kerr to compete with, a very fast talker who always told girls the lies they wanted to hear.

There was a large canning factory, Seabrook, not far from the camp. A foreman from the factory would sneak into camp and pick four of us to work from 7 PM to 11 PM, loading boxes, making sure to get us back before midnight. That gave me extra money to spend and more to send to my parents in Jamaica.

Our morale was boosted by a visit from a distinguished guest from Jamaica, Sir John Huggins, a white Englishman and then Governor of Jamaica. He gave a short speech, encouraging us to keep up the good work, that England was very proud of us, and that we were a tribute to Jamaica. Men pushed and shoved each other to be near him. I wanted a picture with him to send to my mother, thinking how prestigious it would look on her bedroom table. It was like having the angel Gabriel with us. Yet he seemed so simple, dressed in khaki pants and a white short-sleeved shirt with unruly hair. We have never seen those pictures that were promised.

The first time I visited Philadelphia, which was fifty miles away from the camp, Ella Fitzgerald and The Inkspots were performing at the Earl Theatre. I was very fascinated just looking at the tall buildings on Market Street, including Independence Hall and City Hall. I went to a Horn and Hardart restaurant in the City of Brotherly Love. I could choose any menu and sit anywhere I pleased.

After a few visits to Philadelphia, I met a beautiful girl who shared a second-floor apartment with another girlfriend. The first night she took me to her place, her girlfriend was away for the weekend. Just as I had a drink and was preparing for some serious relaxation, the doorbell on the first floor corridor rang three times. The voice that followed was that of her boyfriend/lover, a soldier from Fort Bragg, Georgia, who had come to pay her a surprise visit. She became hysterical, then opened the window and gave me a nod to leap. To tango with a soldier from Fort Bragg was not my cup of tea, so I put my feet out first and gently lowered myself into the shrubberies below, bruising my leg and ripping my pants on the sharp wooden fence in the process. I felt no pain as I made haste to the bus station, only to find out that I had missed the last bus to Bridgeton, but it was a painful experience as I sat waiting for the break of day to catch the first bus back to camp. On the bus I lamented over that missed piece of pie, hoping to try again.

Arriving at camp that early Sunday morning with a part of my pants missing, the guys had a very good laugh, hearing how I got away. Everyone knew that those black soldiers from Fort Bragg were the toughest in the American army. Though I visited that lover many times after that incident, I never attempted to go back to her apartment.

Alfred had the address of an uncle in Baltimore. He invited us for a weekend visit with his family. All three of us caught the Greyhound bus from Philadelphia and headed for Baltimore. We were greeted at McCullough

Street by his uncle, a prominent physician and president of the Baltimore Cricket Association. He was a very pleasant and kind gentleman and a good sportsman. A game of cricket was scheduled at Jude Hill Park, and we were all invited to participate. There were many young, beautiful girls from South Carolina and Virginia working in Baltimore, but I took one look at Sadie and knew in my heart that she was the one for me. Alfred was ahead of the game and had chosen Mary, but Kerr couldn't make up his mind—he wanted them all.

On our way back to Bridgeton, our hearts were filled with the hope of better days to come. On the farm I dreamed of the joy that was waiting for me with that beautiful peach so ripe and so pretty. When I called Sadie on the phone, her voice was music to my ears. Her goodbyes were always sealed with long distance kisses. The promises I made from Bridgeton, so far away, hastened the day of my return. It was a month later when, with great expectation, we three Jamaicans, with hearts strong and valiant, rode the Greyhound back to Baltimore. I was sure that first day blended with the music of the night, love bells would be ringing, much to the delight of my heart.

On my arrival, Sadie was busy packing her suitcase. "I must leave within the hour," her sad voice whispered. "At my mother's side I'll have to be, for she is very ill." Mary, her sister, poured wine, as Alfred and Kerr joined me in lamenting her departure. With a kiss she said gently, "I will return, please wait for me." There was a cricket game at Jude Hill Park, but I couldn't concentrate on the ball as my heart kept floating towards the south, with Carolina on my mind.

Summer had come to an end and the cool breeze of autumn was being felt at night and from the morning frost. The peppers and tomatoes were gone and so were peaches. Our last crops were spinach and apples. The camp managers held a meeting in November. They told us to make a choice to return home to Jamaica for the winter or go to Florida to reap the cane crop in the Everglades. Sure, the cane crop had to be reaped, but I had no experience. To return home would be stopping my monthly contribution. I didn't want to go home, but getting out of the cold was a choice I had to make.

The morning of December 4, 1943, as the train pulled out of Bridgeton, NJ, my name was among the list of 600 or more men. Two days later Azuker, one of the then largest sugar cane plantations in Florida, was our new home. It was warm and humid and far away from the northern cold. The camp was in the middle of thousands of acres of cane fields; only the sky above could be seen. The buildings were high above the ground, erected on posts with steps two or three feet high to keep snakes and water out when it rained.

The following day, three white men arrived. "Welcome to Azuker, boys," they greeted us with southern accents. Several cane fields had been burnt and were ready to be reaped. We were asked to form individual groups of eight men. Every man in the group had to depend on the other to work together as a team. After the process of elimination, eight men were left standing: Alfred and I, with Kerr and five others. We formed our own group, though we had never reaped a cane. We were all taken to a large field, and each of us was given a lasso. Some call it a sword and others, a machete. All the groups were lined up as if to start a race. Bear in mind that cane was sold by the ton. The more tons a group cut, the more they could make. With our lack of experience, we were no match for the men in the other groups. At the end of the week we were placed on the deportation list to be sent back home to Jamaica. The lack of transportation gave us a reprieve, and they placed us on an hourly rate of forty cents. Our new assignment was to burn the cane fields for cutting, pull the weeds, and supplant the fields where needed. My weekly pay was nineteen dollars and twenty cents for six days. The burning of the fields in preparation for cutting was a dangerous job. We would wait for a gentle breeze and then set the field on fire in the direction of the wind. It was pitiful to see the rabbits and snakes and other animals all racing out of the burning field ahead of the soaring flames.

There was a small square in the midst of the huge estate called Peoke. Several black families resided within the areas. Both men and women were bean pickers, and some worked on the sugar estate re-planting cane sucklings. We would walk two miles to this hot spot because girls from Belle Glade would swarm this area on weekends. There was plenty of beer and whiskey with barbeque and fried chicken, and most of the places had juke boxes.

The girls were crazy for the Jamaicans, who would spend their money on them without regret. A group of tough Jamaicans had a fight with a few native men over women. It turned out that the natives were outnumbered and were beaten up. They always sought revenge, but couldn't stop the Jamaicans from coming to the square on Saturday nights. I loved dancing. but on weekends there were just too many slick Jamaicans and not enough girls. Moreover, the girls were always picking the fairer-complexioned guys.

Alfred, Kerr, and I, along with another fellow, chose Tuesday mornings, when possible, to visit Peoke. We had to steal the time from work. The black men were out in the fields picking beans, returning at 1 PM. Monday was a bad day as most of the bean pickers had hangovers from Saturday and Sunday and slept late or just didn't go to work. Once we started up the jukebox, the girls would be on the spot within an hour. They taught us how to dance the Jitter Bug, Suzie Que, Jump and Jive, and the Boogie Woogie. We ate chicken, drank beer, and had lots of fun and made sure to grasp other opportunities that came our way, but always made sure to leave before 1 PM to avoid any confrontation with the men from the bean fields.

Out in the cane fields, the sun combined with the humidity was awful, yet the men were always joking as they leveled the fields of cane, one after the other, and bragged as they worked. One group called themselves the "Eight Army under Montgomery." It became a joke when they confronted a large snake and they all scattered.

Swimming in Lake Okeechobee was a lot of fun. Though rumors of its dangers spread, we always enjoyed every moment.

On April 28, 1944, we left camp Azuker for New Jersey. This time the train had nice passenger cars, much different from the ones that had carried us from New Orleans. Two days later we ended up at Swedesboro, New Jersey, which was a little chilly for me, especially coming from the humidity in Azuker, Florida.

The following day, eight of us were assigned to the Jill Brothers' farm. Asparagus fields were ready, and the tender sprouts had to be reaped without delay. There was no groaning as we tackled the long rows of asparagus. At noon the farmer drove us to Woodstown, a small town nearby, so that we could buy lunch. We all went into a small diner. Our presence was ignored as the two waitresses refused to serve us. One of them went to the kitchen and, within seconds, a large white man wearing an apron appeared and told us to leave. All of us started to curse and swear in our Jamaican patois. Two other white guys joined the side of the owner, and their efforts to get us out only made the matter worse.

Someone called the police, who were not far away, and within minutes, two large pot-bellied officers arrived, their badges plain to see. A look at the broad leather belt around their waists revealed the weapons ready to be drawn. The elder officer was the chief of police. In spite of the commotion, he seemed to be calm.

In a loud voice he said to the owner, "Tony, what the hell is going on here?" The owner answered in a different language, with a few English words. "All right, serve these men and let them get the hell out of here. A war is going on, and I don't want another one in this here town. We were all told to cooperate and I am depending on you to do your share." We were all served and everything calmed down.

As the truck raced back to the farm, we realized that we had received only half of what we'd paid for and felt cheated. It was a way to keep us out and we knew it. Every day we went back to the same diner, but made sure we got our money's worth. The news of the disturbance spread rapidly; all restaurants in the area were ready to take our orders as fast as they could to prevent us from hanging around. They considered their action a war effort and in cooperation with the request of the War Food Administration.

Several hundred acres of land were planted, and canning factories were in full production. Most of the foods were reaped by the bushel or basket. We worked long hours, and our pay increased three hundred or more percent, much to the surprise of the farmers. With speed, we made a lot of money picking tomatoes, peppers, and peas on those large farms. The farmers grieved over the amount of money we were earning. Never before had reapers made such large sums.

To make matters worse, their sons were being drafted and faced dangers on the field of battle. We began to visit Baltimore on weekends, when we were not so busy on the farm. The cricket team, with the older men, was taking a beating from the other teams. With fast bowler Alfred, the wickets started flying, and the team was on the winning track again. Alfred's fastballs were considered flings; they didn't think a small fellow could deliver such fastballs that seldom missed the wickets. The umpire sometimes called them, but we got away with most of those wickets.

My letters to South Carolina went unanswered, but my hope was high as I kept telling myself "the peach" would be sweeter when given more time to ripen. Sadie never returned, but her beautiful sister Marie, with her teasing smile, filled my heart with delight. In spite of my new flame, there was that lingering reminder within my heart for Sadie, *Please wait for me, I will return.* With feelings for two women in my heart, one of which might never be seen again, my heart told me to seek the other one.

I received the sad news of the constant bombings in London and the sinking of many ships all over the ocean. My mother country was taking a pounding. The farm workers effort may have been small, but the strength of those men came from their guts.

I visited a cousin in Philadelphia who was a teacher before he migrated to the United States. He had a prestigious job, working as a manager in the postal system. A black man with such a position during those segregated days was exceptional. He was not impressed with my outfit and frankly told me that a zoot suit did not make me a man. He took me on a tour of Philadelphia and to a Planetarium lecture. I was not moved by his old-fashioned ways, but was very impressed by his knowledge and how the white people called him "Mister." I was happy with my zoot suit and my dancing feet. They went very well with the Jitter Bug and Suzie Que.

The first time I visited New York City from Swedesboro Camp, I was amazed to see the bridges, The Pulaski Skyway, and the entrance to the Lincoln Tunnel. The camp management chartered two trailers with open backs. They placed railings on both sides, the benches bolted down so we could observe the scenery. I was able to see The Empire State Building and the Statue of Liberty from a distance as we passed by.

A game of cricket had been organized at the Triboro Stadium on 125th street in Harlem on July 4, 1944. The Philadelphia cricket club played against a team from the Bronx.

I had the address of a cousin who lived at 141st Street in Harlem. As a young woman, she had visited her parents in Jamaica on many occasions. They were my next-door neighbors. Within an hour, I rang her doorbell. She peeped through a small hole on the door, but couldn't recognize my face or my voice. Then she cracked the door, but was not sure who I was. It took a while to explain that I was a Smikle, the next-door neighbor of her parents in Davyton. She welcomed me inside and explained that her door had many bolts and locks for her safety. She cooked rice and peas with chicken, during which time I had to answer a lot of questions about folks back home in Jamaica and my reason for being in the United States.

On my way back to Triboro Field, she gave me some of the food to take to my friends. The return trip to Swedesboro camp was unforgettable; the drivers raced each other during the night, blowing their horns every time they overtook. Some men sang and made a lot of noise while others slept through the ordeal.

Visiting New York City reminded me of those moments with my cousin, Teacher Haynes, in Philadelphia, which helped me to appreciate new values as I became aware of the arts and culture of a great country. The monuments and sculptures, the flowers around Independence Hall, the marvelous inscriptions so neatly engraved, surely were the work of God manifested by the hands of men. With the war going on, the streets were filled with people, each going his or her own separate way, with one thing in mind–victory!

The cool breeze of November, 1944, set my heart on the Everglades of Florida, but to my surprise, we were transferred to Manville, New Jersey, fifty or more miles further north of where we were. It was a promotion—from the field to the industrial plants.

Alfred, Kerr, and I, with many others, were assigned to work at the Calco Chemical Plant in Bound Brook. Other men worked at Johns Manville. In Manville a new housing project was erected for accommodation of the workers. The people were mostly Polish, Italian, a few Irish, and black. Before the war, blacks were given the most hazardous jobs and mixing with whites was seldom possible. This practice had to be changed since there were many very important jobs, and management had no choice but to fill those positions with us.

Alfred, Kerr, and I were placed in the pharmaceutical division making a white, powdered substance which was sent elsewhere to make sulfathiazole pills. We were given long, white jackets; special caps; and soft shoes. Under the skillful direction of a chemist, we were trained to make batches of powder from various chemicals, making notes of the proportions of each mixture and blending them together in large tanks with agitators turning at specified speeds, while controlling the temperature with crushed ice flakes around the outer space of the tank. It didn't take much time to learn the job, and the supervisors were pleased with our ability to read and make calculations.

I looked like a scientist in the movies: pen in hand, glasses covering most of my face, and always with a notebook. Some of the workers, mostly white women, spoke different languages around us. We knew they were talking about us because they *knew* English, but they weren't accustomed to rubbing shoulders with blacks.

One day a woman looked at me and shook her head sadly. She told me how unfair it was for her son to have to give up his nice job and go to war. She said just seeing us around broke her heart. I sympathized with her and, at the same time expressed to her that my mother cried, thinking that I might not return because of the many evil ways in which black people were being treated in this country by whites. I told her that I hoped her son would soon return.

At Calco I learned to keep my mouth shut about a serious incident involving a group of white women. One day as I was walked towards the men's washroom, the "Women's" was hidden from my view because I walked too closely to the building and the "Wo" of the word "Women" was not visible. As I entered the door at the end of that afternoon's shift, several women were washing up and showering. Suddenly a voice shouted, "Grab him!," followed by other voices shouting, "Grab him!" With lightning speed I disappeared out of sight without being fully recognized. How they wished I'd been caught; they would have had me naked. Though fingers were pointed at me, they were not quite sure. Since they thought we Jamaicans all seemed to look alike, I was not accused. That sign was later extended to avoid further mistakes, but the rumors lingered on.

While at Calco, we were allowed to seek our own lodging. Four of us rented rooms in South Bound Brook from an old lady whose name was Mrs. Blackwell. We called her Mother Blackwell. She cooked and washed for us.

The first time it snowed heavily, in early December, 1944, a Jamaican took a package to the post office in Manville and asked the manager to mail it to his family in Jamaica, West Indies. When asked to declare the contents, the manager was surprised to see he wrote 'real snow' on the declaration form.

That incident was the biggest joke told in bars, churches, and factories all around. Many times I was asked, "Did you hear about the Jamaican who went to the post office in Manville to mail a large package of snow to his family in the West Indies?" I would always answer the same, "Oh yes, he wanted to make sure that his family received that package for Christmas."

I continued to make occasional trips to Baltimore on weekends when the time was available. My new flame was always glad to see me. It was my first winter in the North, so we spent a lot of time indoors.

At the Baltimore Cricket Association clubhouse, I met Uncle Simeon, a short jovial man and a very good sport, for the first time. He had returned from visiting his family in Canada.

At the end of spring, 1945, we were playing a game of cricket at Jude Hill Park. There were three young ladies who were recording the score for the Baltimore team, and one of them caught my attention. I knew that the more runs I scored, the more times my name would be recorded, and she would remember me. Luckily I hit a boundary, and everyone jumped with excitement. Alfred's fastball had those wickets flying, and our team won the game.

At the end of the game, I asked Uncle Simeon to introduce me to the object of my affection. He diplomatically introduced me to all of them. Estelle looked at me with a gentle smile and said, "Hello." I wanted to say a few words to her, but didn't get a chance because her friend Winnie reminded her of some other important engagement they had, and within minutes they were gone. Gazing at the car as it went out of sight, Marie took my hands and said, "Let's go." Mary seemed to have a rope around Alfred's neck.

On our way back to Jersey I couldn't get Estelle out of my mind. The train made lots of local stops, letting soldiers on and off. Their uniforms were shiny and neat. Looking at them I remembered the night that girl gave me the nod to jump through that second floor window. I started to laugh, but Alfred whispered, "Don't laugh at soldiers in uniform unless they give you a joke."

On May 7, 1945, the Germans surrendered. Celebration started the moment the news was announced, but only for a short time, for yet another victory had to be won, as we were reminded of Pearl Harbor. Production continued full speed ahead at Calco. Soon the boys would be coming home to the jobs they once held and to the waiting arms of their mothers and loved ones they'd left behind. My war effort was coming to an end. *Thank God, I could say, Amen!*

Two songs that were very popular then were "When the Yanks Go Marching In" and "I'll Be Home for Christmas." I knew, without a shadow of a doubt, that I, too, would be home for Christmas. I bought a large trunk, the type used by foreigners coming home from abroad, and made a list of names and presents to buy.

Our trips to Baltimore started to bear fruit. Alfred had just received a love letter from Mary saying she'd marry him, and he asked me to be his best man.

"Oh yes, your best man I will be."

On September 2, 1945, the war with Japan came to an end. World War II was officially over. The soldiers were being discharged, and I was prepared to go home.

October, 1945, Alfred and Mary were married. Marie was her maid of honor, and I was his best man. All four of us stood before the minister, and while the couple was repeating their vows, my thoughts lingered on Estelle—would I ever see her again?

The next day I called Uncle Simeon for some help to find her. Two hours later he gave me her address: 940 Harlem Avenue. He reminded me of the myth often repeated by old folks in Jamaica about the smart mongoose, "To steal a chicken, a man must take a good chance." The honeymoon started for Alfred and Mary as Kerr and I returned to South Bound Brook.

Alfred and Mary 1945

During the war, many municipal officials worked part time in factories and other businesses in contribution to the war effort. On the job Kerr bragged to another Jamaican about his romantic activities with a beautiful young girl. An old, white man who was working nearby listened quietly with a smile. Not long after, Alfred and I stood with Kerr as he sadly repeated *his* marriage vows. The parents of the young girl found out that their daughter was pregnant and reported the matter to the police. We went to court with Kerr. He was surprised to see the same old white man that he worked with sitting in the judge's chair wearing a black robe. He whispered to us, "That's the same old white man I worked with." The judge ordered him to get married within thirty days or face prison, and said that if it hadn't been for his war effort, he would have referred the case to the grand jury.

The people of the community treated us better now that the war was over. They all expressed thanks for our services and dedication and also for our good manners, but they were certainly glad that the war was over and wanted us to go home. The officials held a special meeting at the camp, where many praises were heaped on us and speeches of thanks on behalf of the U.S. government were given by an official from Washington.

We left for Camp Murphy in Florida on December 10, 1945, and on December 18th we boarded the SS John L Glen, a transport ship, and reached Jamaica on December 23rd.

My trunk had something for everyone: suits and shoes for my father, dresses for my mother and my sisters, and many other gifts for friends. The merchants and store managers made sure that everything was on sale. All the junk was sold very cheaply to us, anything that looked good. We fell for their tricks. I had problems with my heavy trunks. I received very little help from the other fellows; they had their own overweight luggage issues with which to deal.

I was home for Christmas, having been away for two years, seven months, and eighteen days. Everywhere I went people would say, "Glad to see you, Mr. Man." There were occasional whispers of, "Bra Dog son really look good. *He* is now the big dog." The older men all wanted tobacco money and a drink of rum for Christmas.

Two months later, in 1946, I went to the office of the Minister of Agriculture in Kingston and received a check for 300 pounds, about $1500 then. I immediately bought a Simmons mattress set for my parents and painted the house. My father no longer worked at Cabbage Hall, but continued to farm at Shooters Hill and Virginia.

The New Testament Church of God had doubled its membership, but the Davyton Congregation Church remained the dominant church in the community under the new minister, the Reverend Squire. I went to work at a housing development in Kingston in the area of Jones Town, and with the savings from the farm work, I bought a house at 28½ Mitchell Street. Alfred came to live with me in Kingston while waiting on a visa to return to his wife, Mary. After two weeks on the job, bricks started to sail onto the site from across a high fence. Many fellows in the area were angry because they didn't get jobs in the new development.

The police were called, but as soon as they left, the missiles rained down on us. Fearing I'd get hurt, I left the job and never returned. Alfred received his final papers and visa and left for the United States. As I gazed into the northern skies and watched that plane disappear with my friend Alfred, I thought of those times in Baltimore and pledged to return.

In late 1946, there was a ship leaving for England, and a friend of mine encouraged me to join him on that trip. I had to decline because all my savings had been spent buying the house. I later sold the house and booked my passage for England.

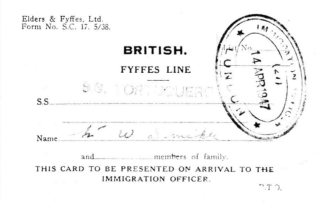

My younger brother George, who was going to school in Kingston and living with me, went back to the country. I informed my parents that I would be leaving for England. My mother took the news very hard and with mixed emotions, and she prayed for my safety every day while I remained with them.

On March 29, 1947, I went to the pier looking for a large, beautiful ship. What I saw was a small, three thousand-ton banana boat called the SS Tortuguero. Seven English and four Jamaicans, including myself, left Jamaica for England. I wasn't happy, but my mind was made up to hit the waves. For seventeen and a half days that small ship glided across the ocean and not a rough sea was experienced. I was all over the ship, from bow to stern, and spent time observing the navigation. There was a small library on the boat, and with time, I found these words:

Ask God to give thee skill in comfort heart,
That thou mayest consecrated be and set apart
Unto a life of sympathy.
For heavy is the weight of ill in every heart
And comforters are needed much, of Christ-like Touch

Author Unknown

I scanned the horizon, fascinated by flying fish. There was not another boat in sight. Though everything seemed beautiful, I was still fearful, remembering from books I'd read of sailors who'd lost their lives in the deep. The boat sailed through the English Channel, up the Thames, and set anchor on the London docks on April 14, 1947. We Jamaicans decided to stick together as a group. We were told to proceed to the Colonial office. A large, white man in full suit with top hat and gloves greeted us warmly. He spoke with an accent, later found to be cockney. I couldn't believe he was a taxi driver. There was a large limousine parked nearby, and he told us he was willing to take us anywhere we wanted to go. One of his friends loaded my trunk into the vehicle. On our way to the Colonial office, he tried to explain to us the route. The other fellows kept quiet, but I asked a few questions. At the Colonial office, we helped him to unload the trunk. The Colonial officers recommended to us the air raid shelter in Clapham Common for lodging. They explained that the shortage of rooms and hotels was caused by the destruction of the city during the bombing of London. The weather was damp and cold, and a shelter two hundred feet underground was an insult from Our Majesty, but we had no choice.

They called a taxi that took us to the shelter. I looked at that trunk with disgust; the guys called it my wife. I started to think of some way to get a divorce from it. The taxi driver suggested that I rent a locker to store it. "A locker?" I asked.

"Oh yes, it's cheaper than paying alimony, only a few pennies per week with unlimited visitation rights," he chuckled. He charged me an extra fare to take me to the lockers.

With only my small hand luggage I was free. There was a small building over the entrance to the shelter that had spiral steps and an elevator. I was surprised to see the large space two hundred feet down at the bottom. There were arched tunnels that stretched in various directions from the large circular space. There were hundreds of people, some with children assembled, eating cakes and tarts, while others drank tea and signed the registry.

Everyone seemed friendly, though some spoke different languages. Those tunnels had rows of four or five bunk beds bolted on the sides with ladders reaching to the top bed, each with three or four blankets neatly folded. I said to my partners, "Buckingham Palace is not too far away, but right now this shelter I must stay." A quick observation showed there were no other blacks around. It has always been comforting for me to see some of my own people wherever I went, but when looking for a job, the fewer the better.

The next day we returned to the Colonial office and were directed to get ration books for distributions of food: tea, sugar, bread, butter, and many other items that were very scarce. Public showers were available all over the city and, for a small fee, with an extra penny for the attendant, who were always white men, he would brush your coat and give you comforting words for the day. The brass rails in these public showers were always clean and polished

We decided to move around in pairs. My companion was a short, fat fellow, Tony, who liked to dress up and use a lot of Khus Khus perfume, the scent of which burned the eyes of everyone. A list of places that needed immediate help was given to us. Our first job was at Steven and Adams in the small county of Wandsworth. They specialized in doors, windows, and wood floors, with parquetry being their specialty. There were immediate openings for the loading of kilns where the wood would be cured. Trucks and lorries from all over England brought the materials to the plant. My resume stated that I was familiar with woodworking and cabinetry, and I was promised a transfer as soon as more help was hired.

On the job all the men wore ties and aprons and were very friendly. We rode the London transport from Clapham Common to Wansworth and had never seen another black person. Since we had no accommodations, each day we had to go to the public showers and then to a restaurant for supper. After five weeks my partner and I found accommodations in West Kensington. It was a large room with two beds.

The landlady used an army blanket to divide the room into two sections. Bed and breakfast with dinner on Sundays was the arrangement. There were two other white men, each with separate rooms. Renting to blacks was a new experience for the landlady, who told us that she preferred to rent it to us than to Europeans.

My first two dreams had come true and I sometimes wondered about the third. A frightening moment came to me one evening as I walked from Steven and Adams to the bus stop. As I gazed upon the bomb blasted city of London; all around me were crumpled bricks. The force of evil spared not even the pinnacle of sacred buildings as they lay among the ruins. Yet long before the evil force struck, the picture of that scenery was placed within my heart; surely another act of God had come true.

London as seen in a dream 1941, revealed in 47

Illustrative drawing of the destruction of London, from my dream.

The Dreams of Youthful Days - Dream #3

Words and Music: Wilbert Smikle

Dreams of Youthful Days was sung when each dream came true, confirming, 'an Act of God.'
To be sung in reverence. All rights reserved.

Dreams of Youthful Days was sung when each dream came true, confirming,
"an Act of God."
To be sung in reverence. All rights reserved.

My partner and I seldom roamed the city of London together. He was too slow getting ready, and I had no patience to wait for him. I visited the West Kensington Congregational Church that was only two blocks away and visible from my residence because most of the buildings in the area were but a pile of rubble. A large part of the church building had been cleared for worship services. They temporarily bricked off a sanctuary and pews. The service was about to begin when I entered the door. One of the ushers handed me a hymnal and showed me to a seat. The hymns were familiar, and my bass voice blended well with the harmony.

MAY 1947

KINDLY LEAVE THIS ORDER OF MORNING SERVICE IN THE PEW.

West Kensington Congregational Church

Castletown Road, W.14.

Minister : Scriptural invitations to worship.
O Lord, open Thou our lips.
Congregation : And our mouth shall show forth Thy praise.
Minister : O God, make speed to save us.
Congregation : O Lord, make haste to help us.
Minister : Glory be to the Father, and to the Son, and to the Holy Ghost.
Congregation : As it was in the beginning, is now and ever shall be, world without end, Amen.
Minister : Praise ye the Lord.
Congregation : The Lord's name be praised.

HYMN.

PRAYER.

General Confession or Thanksgiving
Minister and Congregation.

ALMIGHTY and most merciful Father, we have erred and strayed from Thy ways like lost sheep. We have followed too much the devices and desires of our own hearts. We have offended against Thy holy laws. We have left undone those things which we ought to have done ; and we have done those things which we ought not to have done ; and there is no health in us. But, Thou, O Lord, have mercy upon us. Spare Thou them, O God, which confess their faults. Restore Thou them that are penitent ; according to Thy promises declared unto mankind in Christ Jesu our Lord. And grant, O most merciful Father, for His sake, that we may hereafter live a godly, righteous, and sober life. To the glory of Thy holy Name. Amen.

Program from West Kensington Congregational Church, 1947.

During the announcements I was asked to stand and identify myself. It was a surprise to most of the members to hear a black man from Jamaica, West Indies, who was a member of a congregational church in his country. Everyone seemed anxious to shake my hand at the end of the service. Saturdays were set aside to clear up the bricks and to make more space for worshipping. It was a pleasure to join the group. They served tea, cakes, tarts, and pudding, and it was always a happy moment for me. There was no time to be lonely, as I was invited to join them in many of their social activities, such as going to the local playhouses, hiking, the greyhound dog tracks, dinners, and to the pubs.

In spite of my busy schedule, I found time to visit many of the other places: most of the cathedrals, St. Paul, Westminster Abbey, Hampton Court, the Tower of London, the Botanical Gardens, Albert Hall, Hyde Park, and many other places.

Two infamous dance halls were the popular places around Tottenham Court Road to meet blacks from the West Indies and other countries. Their doors were open seven days per week from 7 PM to 11 PM and 11 PM to 4 AM. Girls from all over London flocked to these clubs seeking love and fantasy. They were crazy for American Jazz and dances.

The drinking, smoking, and loud music in those basements attracted young people from prestigious white families whose parents thought that their children were at skating arenas. Young white men were always jealous to see their white girls releasing their emotions around blacks in the wildest ways. The tribal markings on the faces of some of those young blacks reminded me of those I'd seen in movies of Africa. A black woman was seldom seen at those dances, even though there were a few seen on the streets. In spite of strict surveillance by the bobbies, those hot spots were the center of many skirmishes, white girls defending their black partners when insulted by a white counterpart or rude behavior caused by drinking.

I found a new job at Hampton and Son, a large furniture factory in Clapham. The foreman, whom they called governor, immediately placed me to work in the French polishing room along with six other men. Each had their own separate table. French polishing is a skilled trade which requires experience in shellac hand rubbing. I had done very little French polishing at Holmwood. The foreman asked a young man, who was a helper, to show me the materials. All the polishers worked on four-foot by eight-foot paneling for offices and luxury liners. As soon as the foreman went back to his office, they asked me where in Africa I came from. They were shocked to hear I was from Jamaica.

One of them wanted to know if I had been in the army. I explained that everyone from my country did military work, either producing bullets or other military equipment, and that I had served in the United States in the war effort for two years. There was a roar as they shouted, "He's a jolly good fellow." They took turns showing me the art of French polishing and, though I was slow at first, they encouraged me, and within a month, the foreman informed me that I was fully qualified. I found a new residence at Lilleshall Road that was within walking distance to the job.

News of a black man in the area aroused the citizens; some of them, to my surprise had never seen a black man. In the evenings they lined the sidewalk in front of their homes to get a glimpse of me. Some of them would shout, "God Bless my eye sight."

My earnings were two shillings and a sixpence per hour, or roughly five pounds per week. I was charged thirty shillings per week for lodging that included washing my clothes and dinner in the evening. Every room had a gas heater operated by coins. Gas was limited and rationed. The building had three floors. On the first floor were a bedroom, a large dining room, sitting room, and kitchen. My room was the one on the first floor. My landlady was an English woman who was married to an Irish man whose sister was married to a Scot. She had an eight-year-old daughter. She told me that I was a blessing in the home and that harmony had existed between the mixed families since my arrival.

She had my clothes nicely washed and ironed and made sure my room was cleaned every day. Everyone had to be at the dinner table at 5:30 PM when that bell rang. Afterwards we listened to Scottish and Irish songs and jokes.

I enrolled at Wansworth Technical Institute for a course in building construction. The evening was from 6:30 to 9:00 PM. Sometimes coming home, the fog would be so thick that the conductor on the bus had to walk in front with a lantern for the bus driver to be able to proceed.

I missed Alfred and Kerr and also the good times in Baltimore with the girls. My cousin in Harlem was pleased to hear from me. During the war, she promised to help in my return to the United States. Though I was quite happy, I wanted to be closer to Jamaica, so I reminded my cousin to sponsor me if possible. She told me that jobs were scarce and that men returning from the war were idle. She started on the papers, and within six months I received a permanent residence visa from the U.S. Consulate.

At Hampton and Son I learned to listen to arguments between the younger men and the elderly. They thought I had no idea of the meaning of the profanity they used since I showed no reaction when hearing them. One morning I was late punching my time card and a young woman punched her time card right after I did. The younger men started to tease us as though we had come in late together. That incident led us to becoming very close friends because of the way in that I reacted. She was beautiful and gave me lot of attention. I never stop wondering the *true* reason for her affection.

I encouraged my brother John to join me in England. There were many job opportunities, and the people were warm and embracing. One day I ran head on into a classmate of mine at a London subway station. He was studying law at one of the universities. We exchanged addresses and within minutes joined the crowded train to our separate destinations.

A young student from Nigeria was invited as a guest speaker to the West Kensington Congregational Church. He gave me an invitation to attend a Friday evening dance at the university auditorium. As I was waltzing, a Junior Master, who served at Holmwood when I was a student, brushed against me and said, "Small world. My name is Phillip." At school I had called him *Mr.* Phillip, much to my displeasure. We didn't like to address Junior Masters as "Mister." Both of my Jamaican countrymen wanted to know what I was doing in England, and after telling them that I had been working and going to school, they seemed pleased of my achievement.

Trafalgar Square, London 1947

I discovered that many whites in England had no prejudice against blacks. Most of those whites who lived in colonies under British rule, and had black servants, carried prejudice on their return to England, and they tried to turn their friends and relatives against blacks. They hated to see white women and black men together, even though they were the main perpetrators of miscegenation in the United States.

News of the wedding of Princess Elizabeth to Phillip Mountbatton was circulated all over the world, and London, the center of the celebration, started to dress up in preparation for the great day. All the streets that led to the processional route were being adorned. The light posts and sign posts were given special attention, with a touch of gold, red, white, and blue, and the crown and the lion on every post. The streets were scrubbed and some areas widened.

The Supervisor, also called the Governor, wanted everyone to work on the wedding day. I had no intention of missing this royal occasion, the likes of which might never occur again for me. As the date drew near, people came from all over the empire, and the city of London was jammed. On both sides of the processional streets, they brought beds, chairs, and all forms of comfort in preparation for that great moment.

On November 20, 1947, security was in full force detouring vehicles, barricading off narrow streets, and making sure that the area was clear. The taxi dumped me almost six blocks from the area. I walked and hedged myself through the crowd until I nestled down at Parliament and White Hall, very close to Westminster Abbey. When in a strange place, I always looked around to see if there were any other blacks around. I was the only one in sight. I wore white pants and a white shirt with a cream sweater. A little boy whispered to his father, "Hey, that man needs a shower." His father told him I had just come from the coal mines.

Around 11:20 AM the trumpets sounded for the first procession. Many fainted. The hammock squads (EMS) were there, ready to pick them up and carry them away. There were five limousines in the first processional carrying the queen's mother, Princess Julianne, Prince Bernard, the crowned Prince and Princess of Sweden, and the Duke and Duchess of Manchester. The second processional, of four carriages, carried the King and Queen of Denmark, King and Queen of Sweden, the Queen, and Princess Margaret. The third and final processional consisted of the sovereign escort, followed by the king and the bride. Everything went smoothly, like the ticking of Big Ben. Amidst the joy and exaltation, one could hear small remarks of anger from those who were against the monarchy. I was elated, being it was the most remarkable occasion I had attended in a foreign country.

Kissing my mother on my return to Jamaica from the United States in 1945 was the only occasion that gave me more pleasure. Watching the King escort his daughter in the royal carriage gave me the pleasure of a beautiful reflection.

It was on the 20th of March, 1947, when my daughter was placed in my hands for the first time. She was only three months old. Her name is Cislyn, and she had been born on December 23, 1946. I repeated her name as I gave her a kiss with England on my mind.

Several employees were absent from work the day of the wedding. During work no one talked about the event. As soon as the tea whistle blew, there was jubilation as those who went tried to describe their experience, while some thought the whole idea was totally unnecessary. Then the whistle blew and silence reigned until lunch time. The on and off exaltation and resentment lasted all day. I was asked to give my opinion; after all, some thought I had no reason to be concerned. Telling them where I stood along the processional route shocked them into silence. They never thought I could get so close.

Christmas of 1947 was a series of get-togethers with friends, co-workers, and members of the church. Those moments with my shipmates, Davidson and Tony, along with a few other friends, were moments I would never forget. Enjoying the rice and peas with curried goat or lamb and rum punch, blended with calypso music, made us feel like we were right back in Jamaica.

With winter bearing down, I decided to take it easy. I went to a few shows and movies with church members while making plans to immigrate to the U.S. I submitted my resignation to Hampton and Son, having worked in London for fifty weeks. I had earned three hundred-fifty pounds, nine shillings, and two pence, and I paid twenty pounds two shillings for income tax. My Landlady had a special dinner for me and invited some friends to bid me a happy bon voyage. She adopted my trunk, along with a special embroidered bed-spread that she adored. I thanked the Lord for a wonderful experience and for the many friends I'd made.

On March 21, 1948, I embarked on the SS Marine Flasher at South Hampton and, after a brief stop in Ireland, the ship headed for New York City, across the North Atlantic Ocean. That ship had been built during the war to transport troops to England. The beds in second class were bunks. Once again, I noticed that I was the only black passenger. There were two crew members that were black, and I felt comfortable talking to them. After the first eight hours, all passengers were told to remain below deck as we were encountering a serious storm.

That winter voyage is one I will never forget. The storm raged, and the deck was flooded as the ship was tossed about by the mighty waves of the Atlantic. Passengers were sick and vomiting, and children cried uncontrollably. Like many others, I prayed in silence for the ocean to be calm. They made signs of the cross and uttered prayers to God. The storm lasted four days, after which the sea continued to be rough for two more days, and then there was calm.

Very few of the passengers spoke English, but I enjoyed the last three days with them as they played their flutes and accordions and danced their native dances. Many of the passengers had come from different parts of Europe to South Hampton to board the ship for the journey to the United States.

The dining area that had been abandoned during the storm was now in full service and everyone had a chance to be near each other. I knew we were getting close, but eight days had passed and there was no sign of land, just the wide open sea, and plenty of it. The sight of land had everyone jumping for joy, but that was through very strong binoculars. No land was yet visible to the naked eyes.

At the break of dawn on the tenth day, the shores of America could be seen very far away. An announcement over the ship's intercom said we would be docking at 10 AM. Everyone seemed to take a deep breath; there wasn't much talking as the ship headed slowly towards the shores of New York City. I could see the tall buildings and was able to point out the Empire State Building amidst the early morning haze. The Statue of Liberty stood majestically to the left with her torch held high. Many voices were heard as some passengers pointed in that direction, making sure the children could see the great Lady Liberty.

On March 31, 1948, at 10 AM, the ship docked in the pier around 45th Street. Immigration officers asked us to swear that we were neither communist nor affiliated with communism. Ten days after leaving England, I was back in the United States. "God Bless America," I said silently.

My cousin came to receive me, and soon I was at her apartment at 323 West 141st Street in Harlem. She had a room prepared for me. That same evening she gave me a lecture, saying that I would have to help myself in the kitchen and make sure that everything was clean. We had dinner and chatted for a while. Then she went to bed. I unpacked some of my clothes, took a shower, and relaxed as I silently prayed, giving thanks to God as I fell asleep.

The next morning she left very early for work. I opened the refrigerator and couldn't believe my eyes. It was packed with all kinds of food and drinks. Having lived in London, where food was rationed, the sight of so much food almost caused me to lose my appetite. It was still cold, but the apartment was warm and comfortable. I had to find out where the heat was coming from, so I started looking around and soon discovered radiators.

I was happy to be closer to Jamaica; visiting my parents would cost less, both in time and money. To prevent my mother from worrying, I had not informed her of my intended trip to the United States from England, and now I must inform her of my new address. As I prepared breakfast, the thought of the lecture I'd be getting from her came to my mind.

In London I had been served like a king—funny when you think I was not too far from Buckingham Palace. My English landlady made sure I was pleased. The table was always spread for tea and cake, or lovely plum pudding after dinner.

I had landed in New York with twenty-eight dollars and plenty of hope. Securing a job was crucial; no discrimination or segregation would stop me. I soon found out that a job in Harlem was hard to find, and some jobs required U.S. citizenship or some kind of academic credentials.

With most of the soldiers returning and the slowdown in the production of war materials, I realized that my cousin was right. My financial obligation to Jamaica had to be continued. I went to an employment agency and got a job in Queens as a cabinetmaker in a factory. Getting to work by subway was tedious; the trains were always jammed. I had to deliver furniture all over the city of New York, even though I was hired as a cabinetmaker. It just didn't pay enough money. I started to search for a new job. After three weeks all my funds were exhausted.

In the evenings, with no money, I engaged my time playing table tennis and other games at the 135th Street YMCA. I attended the Grace Congregational Church on West 139th Street in Harlem on the third Sunday after my arrival. My cousin Estelle was a long supporting member of that church, which was only two blocks from her apartment.

The usher asked me to fill out a visitor's card, then took me to a seat. As usual, most of the hymns were quite familiar. During the announcements, the minister told the members he was pleased to introduce Dr. Michael Thompson and Mr. Wilbert Smikle, two distinguished visitors from London, England. Though he read the names of other visitors, Dr. Thompson and I received the loudest applause. He told the members that I was a cousin of Miss Sewell, one of the pillars of the church.

During the sermon my thoughts were in silent prayer asking God to help me in finding a job; I really didn't digest much of the sermon. After the service was over, Dr. Thompson came to me, shook my hand, and asked me what business took me to England from Jamaica. I told him that I was pursuing a course in building at the Wansworth Technical Institute and working at the same time. He asked me to visit him at the YMCA, where he was staying temporarily.

On Tuesday evening of that same week, while playing table tennis at the YMCA, I felt a gentle touch on my shoulder. Dr. Thompson was passing by and asked me to join him for dinner. He was surprised when I declined, not realizing that I had just eaten. He then asked me to have a drink, gave me two dollars, shook my hand, and left. I was down to my last two dollars and was quite serious about finding a new job.

Now with that extra two dollars, I immediately left for home and made plans to travel to Calco Chemical in Bound Brook, New Jersey, and apply for a job. The bus that took me to Bound Brook cost me one dollar and forty cents. Calco Chemical was where I had worked during the war.

At Calco I was told to return in three months. Remembering that Jamaicans had worked at Johns Manville, another large company in the area, I took a bus there for twenty cents and filled out an application. The employment manager was very kind and told me to return the following day for a physical.

According to my calculations, I had only forty cents left. As I stood at the bus stop, the day shift crew was coming out of the main gate at 3:30 PM. I was fascinated to see those men hurrying to catch the local bus, some driving their cars. Others who lived in the borough of Manville and near to the plant were walking, and no one seemed to notice me. My eyes peered to catch a glance of a black person, but there were none in sight.

Suddenly I recognized a Jamaican heading towards the bus stop and realized that I had worked with him during World War II at Calco. His name was George, and he had not returned to Jamaica with us after the war because his girlfriend would not let him go. So he went to Johns Manville and got a job. He approached me, and we renewed our acquaintance.

He encouraged me to join him in Somerville, which is two miles away, rather than returning to New York City that evening. On our arrival, he introduced me to his landlady, Ms. Brown, at 27 Franklin Street. She rented me a room for seven dollars per week and told me that she would wait for my first paycheck for the money. George had developed a southern accent that was very difficult to understand. Many thought he was an American. That same evening he took me to a local diner on Main Street, and with a special card issued by the diner he purchased dinner for both of us.

The next day I returned for the physical and started to work at Johns Manville, on April 24, 1948, at a rate of $1.17 an hour. Johns Manville had about twenty-five hundred employees, most of them on one of three shifts because many of the operations ran twenty-four hours around the clock. The huge plant had many large brick buildings with railway lines criss-crossing all over. Many of the raw materials had to be delivered by railway cars and trailers.

In those early days after the war, there was only a small percentage of blacks, most of them unloading raw materials from train cars or loading finished products and dumping bags upon bags of dusty materials in the warehouse and the main buildings, the most hazardous work. Inside the plant was very hot and dusty with all kinds of fumes, in spite of the many blowers to purify the air.

Most of the people who worked at the plant were Americans of Polish, Italian, Irish, and Slovak decent. Some of them had nicknames and didn't care to rub shoulder to shoulder with blacks. They all seemed to be very happy working at Johns Manville, which offered them security and a future pension.

I started to work in the roofing department where asphalt roofing of all descriptions was made, along with asphalt rolls. This department employed about two hundred-fifty men. Each of the five machines covered a distance of about one thousand to fifteen hundred feet and were six to ten feet wide.

The loading areas were the beginning of all operations, followed by the saturation tank and asphalt and granular area, the cooling and looping area, then the cutting, packaging, and stacking areas. The easiest jobs were in the saturation, asphalt, and granular applications. Those areas had a clique of white men with ten to fifteen years seniority. The dust and fumes in those areas was very thick, even with several exhaust fans. Those men worked together and made sure only replacements of their choice were welcome.

They smoked cigars and cigarettes, and their complexions were black from the fumes and dust. I was given a job in the cutting area, quite a simple task, clearing jams from under the cutting machines.

There were two other blacks; one dumped dust in a large asphalt tank and the other stacked finished products. For the first three months I cleared tabs and stacked finished products. One night the cutter operator did not check the dimensions of each shingle as often as required, and three hundred squares were rejected for being off size. The next morning the superintendent was furious and ordered the midnight foreman to have me measure a shingle every half hour and report the dimension to the cutter operator and, at the same time, clear tabs. They gave me a tape measure with a note pad and pencil for recording the dimensions. Any deviation of size had to be reported to the cutter operator without delay. The cutter operator had eighteen years seniority on the job.

A week later, a white fellow who worked for the Underwriters Lab was placed on the midnight shift with me. His job required that he measure the dimensions of each shingle every hour and to test the specifications for the underwriter's report. He had been sleeping on the job, and every morning he checked *my* record to complete his report. One morning I jokingly hesitated to give him my record. He became very angry and, in his attempt to snatch it away, called me a nigger.

I pushed him away. The huge fellow started to throw rights and lefts in my face. I covered as much as I could to prevent the blows, then I threw a hard left to his face as he was moving in on me. It caught him right in his eye.

At that moment they stopped the fight and everyone kept that incident quiet to prevent him from getting fired. He wore a black eye for more than two weeks. A white bully wearing a black eye given by a "Ju-ma-kee," as I was called, was an embarrassment. He threatened to get even with me, but never followed through. To ease his embarrassment, I told him it was just a lucky punch.

A white man who had been stacking shingles bid for a higher paying position. They gave me the stacking job after no other with seniority showed any interest. It was permanent, and though tough on my back, it gave me the privilege of being part of the crew on the prestigious number four machine. The area was warm in the winter, and the air less contaminated with dust and fumes.

I became a member of the labor union and sometimes worked overtime when my release man failed to show up for work. On the easier jobs, overtime was hard to get. Favoritism by the foreman was prevalent and caused several grievances to be filed.

The opportunity to save was encouraged by joining the credit union through payroll deduction.

My good friend George went on leave and never returned to Somerville or to the job. Not long after, another Jamaican from Brooklyn came to work at Johns Manville and needed a place close by to stay. I took him to Somerville, and my landlady rented him a room. We worked together for many years.

In June of 1948, I visited Baltimore for the first time since 1945. I had two lovers on my mind; Marie, who was waiting for me, and Estelle, who'd had no thought of me since she had only seen me on two occasions. Alfred and Mary, with their two children, were living on Carey Street. They, along with Marie and several friends, gave me a warm welcome. The good old days of eating, drinking, and dancing overwhelmed everyone as the evening filled our hearts with pleasure. Amidst the joy and celebration, the torch that burned within my heart for Estelle glowed brighter, and the eagerness of seeing her propelled my imagination to find a way.

The next day I decided to visit Uncle Simeon in East Baltimore. Marie wanted to accompany me, but Mary reminded her of a previous engagement involving Alfred, who would drive them. At Uncle Simeon's place I called Estelle, who hung up at the sound of my voice. She had no idea who I was. On my second attempt, her mother answered the phone and asked me to wait. Estelle picked up the phone and listened as I tried to explain who I was. "It has been a long time and the memory of our acquaintance has completely left my mind," she said.

"If only I could see you again," I said. "After all, I have traveled many thousands of miles through distant countries just to see your beautiful smile once more." She agreed to see me within the next two hours. As I rang the doorbell at 940 Harlem Avenue, her mother opened the door slightly, took one look at me, then closed the door and walked away. I looked towards the sky in desperation. The third floor window was open and there she was, looking down at me with that beautiful smile. My heart skipped a beat as I lifted my fingers to my lips and issued her a kiss. Then, in a whisper, I gently asked, "Will you be mine?" She did not say a word, so I waved goodbye and walked away. As I headed toward the intersection, a warm feeling of joy filled my heart with the assurance that certainly she was my ideal, the one of my dreams, the one of pure divine. I went back to Carey Street to bid Alfred and friends goodbye. I thanked them for a warm welcome and a lovely and enjoyable time.

Stacking shingles every day was backbreaking work, especially when the machine speed was increased for more production. Of course more production meant more bonuses; sometimes the weekly salaries were increased more than 100 percent. I applied for a new position that had opened. This job was much easier. In spite of my seniority, the job was given to a white man with less seniority who had gained qualification in an unscrupulous way. As a member of the union, each employee had the right to bid for a job. Eligibility called for seniority or qualification. That had prevented many blacks from gaining higher paying jobs, or those with better working conditions. White employees would use every spare minute, including lunch period, to show their friends with less seniority how to perform a more favorable job, especially on the midnight shift, when there were less supervisors. When a position became available, a white was usually selected, as long as he had *some* qualification, thus circumventing seniority procedures.

The system worked well until it started to affect whites. It took many years for the union and the company to comply with new civil right laws that called for equal opportunity employment for all. That clause, which had hurt many blacks for a long time was changed to read, "highest seniority with time allowed to qualify," which meant *any* employee with seniority must be given time to learn the job and to be qualified.

My folks in Jamaica were happy knowing that I was now living in America. Mother and dad were keeping well and received a letter from me each month. I corresponded with my seven brothers and sisters, each individually, and as often as necessary, and encouraged them to prepare for the opportunity of migrating to America.

In my first letter to Estelle, I expressed the joy within my heart when gazing towards the sky and suddenly caught her beautiful smile at the window. How I wished to be near her, to touch her lovely hands. Her reply was short, but reassuring, that a next visit, without a zoot suit, might be more favorably accepted by her mother.

My Uncle Simeon had an accident on his job and was recuperating at home. I made a second visit to Baltimore in July of 1948. Instead of staying at Alfred's place, I decided to stay with Uncle Simeon in East Baltimore and take a taxi to see Estelle. Her parents were expecting me, and this time I wore a new straight conservative suit.

I rang the doorbell and her mother, who was in the kitchen, called her down from the third floor. She came down and gave me a warm welcome, then introduced me to her father, who was sitting in the living room. Her mother came from the kitchen, shook my hand, said a nice hello, looked me all over with a smile, and asked to be excused and returned to the kitchen. Estelle stood with me for a while, then also asked to be excused and went to the kitchen. I was left sitting there with her father, who had piercing eyes with a gentle smile. He began to ask me several questions about Jamaica and gave me the impression that he knew a lot about the island. He couldn't understand why I had gone to England and thought I had been in the British Army during the war. He showed me pictures of his two sons that had served in the navy and in the army during the war. Their uniforms were decorated with ribbons, and I could tell he was very proud of them.

I told him that during the war I had worked for the USA Food Administration, which was responsible for supplying food and war materials to the men on the battlefront. I explained that without that very important role our men in the field would have had a very hard time with empty stomachs and no bullets. Estelle's mom offered cakes and coffee, which gave me a break and made me feel more at ease.

Estelle's friend Winnie called and asked her to bring me over to her place for a short while. I was glad to be away from her parents and for the opportunity to put my arms around her, look in her eyes, and maybe get a kiss. While Winnie prepared dinner, her boyfriend came over and started to play some soft music. Estelle joined Winnie in the kitchen while we got acquainted and had a few drinks. It was an enjoyable evening as we sat, ate, drank, and danced the time away. Upon reaching home, she asked me to stay for a while. Her father and mother were in bed, so we sat in the living room and talked, then we hugged and kissed for the first time. She asked me to return the next day at 2 PM for dinner.

The taxi arrived and, with one last kiss, we bid goodnight and I headed to East Baltimore. The next day I visited Alfred and Mary, hoping to tell Marie it was over with us. First they wanted to know why I hadn't stayed at their place. They had no idea that Uncle Simeon was sick and was very surprised to hear the news. Marie did not show up to greet me, and I became curious, only to be told that she had left two days before for South Carolina and that she had tried to call me but had been unsuccessful. I stood there quietly for a while, thinking that they were joking, and that she would surprise me. Sure enough she was away to see her mother who had been ill. It would have been very difficult to end our relationship after hearing the sad news of her mother's illness. I felt a moment of grief as I offered my regrets, but refrained from making any further comment, remembering Sadie's unfulfilled promise to return.

Remembering the two o'clock dinner appointment, I said my goodbyes and headed east to Estelle's home. I bought a half-dozen roses for Estelle, a box of candy for her mother, and a box of cigars for her father. Dinner was delicious. Her mother was pleased as I praised the hands of the lovely cooks, to which her father agreed by saying, "That's the reason I married her."

After dinner her father went for a nap while her mother insisted on cleaning up the kitchen. Estelle and I sat in the living room looking over the family album. She was the youngest of seven children, and her three brothers and sisters were all married. She had recently graduated from the Cortez Business School and was a teacher living at home with her parents. One of her sisters was married to a Jamaican, a well-known florist in the Baltimore area, which was probably why her father had asked me all those questions about the island.

The time for my departure was getting close. I gazed at the high third floor window of Estelle's bedroom and wondered if it would be possible to sneak by the second floor bedroom of her parents at a later date. *Don't even think about it,* I said to myself. She gave me one last kiss, which was short, and whispered "Please return very soon." I bid her mother goodbye as I looked up again at Estelle's bedroom before I left for home.

Uncle Simeon was relaxing as I stepped in the door to say goodbye and prepare for my trip back to Jersey at 6 PM. He was pleased to learn of my accomplishments and warned me not to screw up. I gave him a broad smile as I entered the taxi and left for the train station.

I couldn't stop thinking about the pictures in the album; Estelle's family was good looking, right down to her grandmother. I could hardly wait to get back to Somerville and take a good look in the mirror.

I grinned at myself and checked my dentures for imperfections. I was falling in love; Estelle was everything I'd hoped for, a beautiful rose shimmering in the fresh morning dew. For Maryland, a prince had given up his crown for the one he loved. *I too must make so humbly, yet so sure. A modest commitment to my parents I may not break, though a vow to forsake, I am sure to take, that decision my God I ask of thee to make.*

My landlady invited me to join a group of friends for a trip to the beautiful Rye Beach in New York in August, 1948. With many beautiful girls around from which to choose, she was surprised that I chose to invite Estelle. It was quite sudden, and a surprise, so she asked if she could respond to my request the following day. I was asked to reserve a hotel for her in the area for two days. Though there were many rooms available in the hotels at Somerville, they refused my reservation. My landlady, knowing the reason, suggested allowing Estelle to use her bedroom for two nights, providing I didn't share it with her. It was an unbelievable sacrifice.

That warm Friday evening before the trip, I escorted Estelle from the New Brunswick train station to Somerville. She was beautiful, her smile warm and gentle.

I introduced her to my landlady, who welcomed her warmly and showed her to the bedroom, which was beautiful.

The next day three buses left, arriving at the beach at around 11:30 AM. I changed into my swimsuit as fast as I could and waited to get a glimpse of Estelle in hers. She was breathtaking, as pretty as could be. We went sailing in a row boat for two. I had never been in one before. Though the water was calm, I was no master rower, and we just kept going around and around in circles. Finally, I decided to just let it drift, then with gentle strokes, we were moved along merrily, following our own course, away from the laughter and excitement of the other lovers as they kissed and sailed along.

Rye Beach

After I brought the boat into port, Estelle wanted to ride the roller coaster. I recalled how that "devil" had frightened me in London, but without hesitation, we were on our way. It was fun. We joined a few of our busmates for lunch and, after refreshing ourselves on the beach and swimming in the cold water, it was time to depart. We reached home at 10:30 PM. I couldn't sleep that night and neither could Estelle. We finally decided to meet halfway, which proved uneventful for the purpose I had in mind. It was then that she promised to fulfill our desire on my next trip to Baltimore.

Sunday morning the smell of bacon and the sounds of laughter alerted me to breakfast. Arriving downstairs, Estelle, the landlady, and two friends welcomed me to the table. Estelle had joined the group to prepare breakfast while I slept. At 2 PM I took her to the train station and, after a few kisses, watched her train slowly roll away.

In 1945, while Alfred, Kerr, and I were working at Calco Chemical in Bound Brook, we lived at the home of Miss Blackwell on Warren Street in South Bound Brook. I paid her a visit for the first time after I returned in 1948. She encouraged me to rent an apartment from her. My old schoolmate Kerr was back in Jamaica and things were not going well. He'd spent all his farm work money in the furniture and building trade. I received a letter from him asking that I contact his wife, whom he'd left in 1945 after the war, to sponsor his return so that he could be able to support his only child. Though she had not heard from him, she agreed. I helped her secure all the necessary immigration documents and he received a visa. After lending him some money, he returned in April of 1949.

In June of 1950, I visited my cousin in Harlem by bus right after the Friday evening shift, reaching New York City at 12:30 AM. I was walking on 141st Street, heading from Seventh to Eighth Avenue that early dismal night. Two men were fast approaching from behind. They moved rapidly and spoke with rough voices. I kept glancing over my shoulder, not paying attention as I tried to cross Eighth Avenue. Suddenly someone shouted, "Look out, man!" One more step and I would have been mowed down by a speeding taxi. "Are you crazy man?" asked the other as they both went by. Embarrassed, I thanked them and said a silent prayer.

In August of 1950, I purchased my first car, a 1946 Dodge, for six hundred dollars with a down payment of three hundred. I received my driver's license a month later and decided to drive alone to Baltimore, which is approximately two hundred miles away from South Bound Brook. Two days before, I went over the route carefully, making note of the various towns and highways. I left on Friday at 11:30 PM, right after work.

After passing through Trenton; the route takes on the name Roosevelt Boulevard, and when I got to Philadelphia, I had to get directions to get out of the city. In Delaware, Route 1 disappeared completely as the highway assumed different names. After leaving Wilmington, the highway became darker as the streetlights were spaced farther apart in the country. I saw a vehicle with a Maryland license plate traveling ahead, so I decided to follow at a distance, hoping it was heading for Baltimore.

With my eyes focused on the vehicle ahead, I didn't notice when the highway veered off in two directions. After about forty minutes, the vehicle turned off the highway and headed towards a farm house. I turned around a short distance ahead, to avoid suspicion, and continued back towards the intersection where the road divided and took the highway south. Gas was getting low as I headed along, not sure if the direction was the right one. I came to a gas station at an intersection where several trailers were filling up by a small diner with a few men drinking coffee. I had my tank filled and my water and oil checked. The attendant noticed my license plate and asked where I was going. He was kind and instructed me to take Route 40, which was fifteen miles east. Baltimore was approximately eighty miles south.

Route 40 was a much better highway. It was wider and had more traffic. Soon the signs of popular towns appeared, such as Aberdeen and Fullerton. I knew that Baltimore was not far away. It was 7 AM Saturday morning when I rang the doorbell of Uncle Simeon. He couldn't believe I had taken such a chance driving alone in the middle of the night. He warned me of what *could* have happened. If my car had broken down in a dark area out in the wilderness, as a black man I might never be heard of again. I had no fear and didn't think being black was a problem. A man in love is sometimes blind to danger.

My only concern was getting a shower and some sleep. At ten that morning I called Estelle. She thought I was still in New Jersey, but was assured I was on my way and would arrive at 11 AM. I took the car to a nearby car wash, and those guys did a wonderful job.

There were no parking spaces in front of Estelle's home, but a space across the street gave a nice view of my car. At noon I rang her bell. My darling opened the door and greeted me with a kiss. It was long. Her mother was ill and in bed. Her father was at work. The long silence after the door was answered caused her mother to inquire if everything was all right.

I had planned to surprise Estelle with my new car. She didn't know that I had driven down and asked from which station I'd made the call. I opened the door and showed her the new car on the other side of the street. Instead of complimenting me for such a daring achievement, she echoed some of the same dangers Uncle Simeon had pointed, adding, "I love you, just think what could have happened to you." She went across the street and checked the car out, telling me how nice it was.

Her mom was unable to leave her bedroom, so Estelle made lunch and brought it to her. Her mom peeped from the door and said hello. Estelle told her that I had driven down alone during the night and was staying with my uncle in East Baltimore.

Uncle Simeon called to let me know that he would be out of town for the weekend and would return on Sunday evening. Estelle and I decided to visit Winnie and have dinner at a nice restaurant. Estelle reminded me that since her mom was ill, she wanted to be back home by 10 PM. After dinner, I took Winnie home, and then headed straight for Uncle Simeon's place. Estelle was nervous, but I told her we would be safe and alone, that Uncle Simeon would not be back until Sunday evening. We were alone for the first time. The joy and pleasure in each other's arms, the ecstasy that could have lasted all night, came to an end when she reminded me that she needed to be home by 10 PM.

Her father was home and was very glad to see me. After staying with her in the living room for a short while, I bid her goodbye with a gentle soft kiss and went back to East Baltimore. On Sunday morning I drove over to see Alfred and Mary. Marie had since returned from South Carolina and had heard about my new flame. She told me how much she respected our friendship, but was uncertain because I had never nurtured the relationship for it to grow. She held no bitterness and seemed to be just as warm as always. She also revealed that she had fallen in love with someone else.

Howard, the grandson of Cousin Caroline, the lady who was generous and kind to me while a student at Holmwood, was living with his mother on Convent Avenue in Harlem. He had a job in downtown New York City that he didn't like. Due to my knowledge of Bound Brook, Plainfield, Somerville, and Manville, I suggested that he join me in New Jersey to find a better job. He was not quite sure if the idea was a good one, so I left him my address in South Bound Brook and told him how to find me, should the occasion become necessary. One day he suddenly showed up.

I introduced him to my landlady, who prepared accommodations for him. Knowing that he had learned to do machine work at Holmwood, I decided to take him to Mack, the motor company in Plainfield. Though I worked at Johns Manville, I felt that Mack Motors was a better and cleaner place that paid more money. Segregation was still rampant, and though they were hiring, they refused to give him a job. The following week I took him back, and they refused to hire him. He asked me to take him somewhere else, to which I agreed. On our way to this other place I turned around and went right back to Mack Motors and begged him to try one more time, telling him I'd pick him up later. I was working on the afternoon shift and was furious that he wasn't there when I went to pick him up. Returning to Bound Brook, I saw him alight from a bus, then show me his badge to start working the following day. He was the only black holding the position of a machinist in the Plainfield Mack Motor Company, the first to be hired in that position. His pay was twice as much as he would have received had I taken him to work at Johns Manville, where they would not have given him that position as a new employee.

Not long after, a fellow Jamaican named John came to work at Johns Manville. He stood at the main gate waiting to get a glimpse of someone who might be able to assist him in finding lodging in the area. I took him to Bound Brook where a lady who had a boarding house in the close proximity to my residence rented him a room. We became friends. Howard and John were very impressed with the picture of my darling Estelle, which was proudly displayed on my bedroom table. They were encouraged by my success and decided to invade the city of Baltimore with the hope of a lover each to find.

Alfred and Mary welcomed the new invaders, who he knew, and a party was set in motion.

Estelle clung very close to me, her affection clear to see. My friends made sure to look the other way. There were many girls of pure delight, all like roses in a garden. Howard's eyes caught Ruth, a gift from heaven sent. As we sped back to New Jersey, I was sure that Maryland was indeed the home where lovers' hearts are taken. Even a prince, with all his power, could not resist.

Estelle's mother became seriously ill and died within a short time. I took a week from the job to be with the family. Everyone had a chance to meet me. Though my mood was subdued by the sad occasion, they all embraced me as a member of the family.

I spent most of my time with Estelle and some of her brothers and sisters as we became more acquainted. She was the only one living with her father. We would join Howard, John, and Alfred at the cricket games that were played at Jude Hill Park.

On one of my visits, I took her class ring, which she missed but said nothing. On March 3, 1951, I asked her to marry me. Without answering, she showed me her manicured fingers, and as I reached for the engagement ring, she said, "Yes." With a kiss I placed the ring on her finger. She took my hand and led me to her father to show him the engagement ring, then she said, "Ask of my father."

I nervously asked him for her hand in marriage, but before I could finish, he said quietly, "To give of my daughter is to give of my heart, but you seem to be the one." She hugged her father and he shook my hand.

On one of her visits, my landlady introduced Estelle to a young lady who sang metso soprano with the Bound Brook Community Chorus and the Metuchen Choral Society. Her name was Mary Holzendorf. They immediately became friends and, as a result, I became involved in classical music and was a regular guest at their concerts whenever she performed in the area. The news of our engagement spread among many relatives and friends in Baltimore. Mary and Miss Blackwell gave Estelle a bridal shower in South Bound Brook, and many friends from New Jersey and New York were invited.

The wedding date was set for July 29, 1951, at the Metropolitan AME church in Baltimore. During the engagement we found an apartment in Elizabeth, New Jersey, and furnished it in preparation for residency after the wedding. The blessed day finally came and a wedding party of twelve including my best man Alfred, three ushers (Howard, John, Winnie), three bridesmaids, and the bride's brother Charles, stood by my side. It was strictly formal with tuxes and tails. Her father escorted her down the isle and placed her hand in mine. The Reverend Kelly Jackson, with solos by Mary Holzendorf, who sang "Ava Maria" and "Jesus, Joy of Man's Desire," reverently joined us together in holy matrimony.

The local newspaper did a fine job covering the event. Most of my relatives and friends from the New Jersey and New York areas attended the ceremony. Uncle Simeon decorated the banquet hall beautifully. We had our honeymoon in Asbury Park at the Carver Hotel.

Mary Holzendorf

Estelle and her father

Wilbert and Estelle's Wedding Photo

The Baltimore Afro-American, August 18, 1951

Smikle-Cummings Wedding Ceremony in Baltimore

Mr. and Mrs. Wilbert Smikle who were married in Baltimore, Sunday, are shown with members of the wedding party, left to right: Howard Hall, Charles B. Cummings Jr., John Smith, Alfred Williams, Mr. and Mrs. Smikle, Charles B. Cummings S., Miss Lillie Carter, Miss Winifred Parris, Mrs. Margaret Moore, Mrs. Grayce Booth, Miss Thelma Barnett; and at front, Beverly Jean Booth. Mrs. Smikle is the former Miss Estelle O. Cummings. The bridegroom is a resident of South Bound Brook, N.J.

Newspaper Article of our Wedding.

Wilbert and Estelle arrive in Elizabeth, NJ after honeymooning in
Asbury Park.

On August 5, 1951, we moved into our newly furnished apartment at 414
Elizabeth Avenue in Elizabeth, New Jersey, that was very close to the Greystone Presbyterian Church. Estelle, an AME Methodist, and I, a Congrega-
tionalist, became members of the Greystone Presbyterian Church by the
affirmation of faith and had our first communion on Good Friday night service in 1952.

In my absence, Howard and John continued their occasional trips to Baltimore. I missed the pleasure and fun of riding with them, but I had become
active in civil rights and church matters on weekends.

Eight months after our wedding, Estelle and I, along with many friends
and relatives, stood with Howard and Ruth as they repeated their marriage
vows, after which they moved to Somerville, New Jersey, and settled down.

Howard and Ruth

John, who hadn't been able to make up his mind on a Maryland woman, was easily hooked by a beautiful Jamaican lady named Pat. We attended their wedding, and they settled in New Brunswick.

All three of us were now married men, living within twenty minutes of each other. The wives became very close friends and made sure to keep the ties that bound us together as tight as possible. Sometimes it was difficult to differentiate whose wife belonged to whom. We never forgot our friends in Baltimore and sometimes made group trips to be with them at crab festivals and many other affairs.

Estelle and I found a new apartment in Edison Township in an area called Potters' Crossing. This new location was closer to my job and the route had less traffic. Potters' Crossing was a small village district that had a railroad crossing at Inman Ave. There was a train platform and several large buildings at the intersection. Not far away was the Potters' Farm Homestead and the Sun Valley Farm Restaurant and Hotel. Further to the east were groceries and general stores, surrounded by large homes, churches, salons, pool halls, the fire station, and the North Edison Civic Improvement Association. A small section of the open area was occupied by squatters who built shacks and on the weekends gambled and sold corn whiskey and barbecue, which sometimes caused disturbances.

I became a U.S. citizen in 1954 and joined with the North Edison Civic Improvement Association, a local black organization in the area that worked with the local police and Edison City Council to help eradicate the violence on weekends.

My mother became seriously ill. Estelle, who didn't care to fly, decided to remain at home. It was my first flight out of Idlewild Airport (now JFK International) on board Avianca, a South America airline. I landed in Miami and, after a delay of two hours, continued onto Jamaica.

Mother Smikle, as everyone called her, had made a slight improvement, and seeing me for the first time in seven years brought her renewed strength. My father's health was failing also, but he flexed his muscles, reminding me of an expression from the old days that said "two bulls can't reign in the same pen."

My brother John had migrated to England, David was doing most of the farming, and my sisters—all out of mom's control—were behaving well, serving the Lord in the New Testament Church of God.

Mother wanted to know about my wife. They looked at the wedding pictures and wanted to know when they'd have more grandchildren. They came to the conclusion that my wife was a lovely woman and had taken good care of me. Mother was very happy for me and said, "My prayers have been answered."

The house had been painted and all the stones had been white washed, but the old road remained the same; it had not been widened or improved for automobile access. Most of the older folks still called me "Mr. Man" and wanted their Christmas gifts. Money was scarce, but five shillings went a long way. Going home at Christmas was very costly; Mother and Father and all my sisters and brothers had to be remembered, each with a gift.

Estelle helped in selecting gifts for the women, including my mother. I made sure my father received a new suit and a pair of shoes, the other men pants and shirts. I was happy to see the improvements made by my financial commitment over the many years. A new addition and re-roofing had made the old house more attractive and accommodating.

On my first Sunday worship at the Davyton Congregation Church after many years, the Minister announced my appearance to the congregation as "Mr. Man." Someone forgot to inform him of my correct name. I was pleased with the congregation's applause as I told them of my true identity. My parents' church had regular nightly meetings with a lot of young people singing, clapping, praising God, and crying out, "Hallelujah." My visit seemed to set them on fire, as they all shouted and called me "Mother Smikle's son, Mr. Man."

Every available area of our property, was prepared and planted with crops of corn and peas, giving some of the men a chance to earn a few shillings. Those who had no jobs were encouraged to follow my footsteps and try and get to America on the farm work program, which did not end after the war. The need for farm workers grew stronger every year.

My parents prayed for me and asked the good Lord to be with me always. I left Jamaica on December 31, 1954, at 10 PM, arriving at Idlewild at 6 AM January 1, 1955. I was happy to be back at home with Estelle, who had missed me very much. During my absence, two of her nieces from Baltimore spent Christmas with her.

When my father-in-law became ill, Estelle took time off from her job to be with him for a while and help one of her sisters who had returned home after the passing of their mother. He died not long after. Estelle and the rest of the family took his death very hard.

In 1956 my wife and I purchased a building lot approximately three-quarters of a mile east of the Urban Development area of Edison. The area was zoned Residential B for the erection of buildings on a quarter-acre lot. We secured an architectural drawing for a house and applied to the township for a building permit. The building inspector, who knew us because of our involvement in the North Edison Civic Improvement Association, was very cordial and suggested that we first secure a mortgage and return in three months and a permit would be ready. Several banks turned down our request for a $13,000 construction mortgage. The attorney who did the closing of the purchased property requested a fee to represent us for the construction mortgage. Within three months, the Robert Treat Savings and Loans of Newark granted us a mortgage.

On our second request for a building permit, we were shocked when told by the building inspector that the area had been re-zoned from Residential B to Residential A and that the requirement was changed from quarter-acre to half-acre for each building lot. What they didn't say was that the area was called the Highland Subdivision for Caucasians only and that blacks should live somewhere else. Most of the land in the area was wooded, undeveloped, and owned by the township. We went back to the attorney who helped us in securing the mortgage. With his instruction we were able to purchase the quarter of an acre lot adjoining ours, thus conforming to the new zoning order of a half-acre.

On our third attempt, with two titles in hand representing a half-acre, our presence was ignored. After waiting for an hour, my wife, who is usually quite calm, became enraged at the way we were being treated. She said loud enough for them to hear, "They were always so nice when our *votes* were needed; how shameful it is that they ignore us when we need their service."

The mayor, who was in his office and heard her, said, "George, see what you can do to help these people."

George answered, "But Tony, we can't help them. They are here seeking a building permit to erect a house on a quarter of an acre, which is now been re-zoned for a half-acre."

At that moment I interjected with my hand in the air, showing them that we had secured a half-acre to meet the new requirements of the zoning board. The sound of my voice and the waving of the titles caught them by surprise, and after a brief silence, the mayor asked to see the architectural drawing of the building. Upon observing it, he said, "George, this is what we want in that area." He then turned to us and asked, "Can you folks afford to build such a large house?"

I told him I was a builder and had already secured a mortgage. The building inspector pointed out that the drawing would have to be changed to conform to specification. The frontage would have to be reduced, and two families were not allowed.

"Let's help them to secure a variance," said the mayor.

They asked us to contact Mr. Simon, secretary of the zoning board, to get all the necessary documents with instructions on securing a variance. The permit called for the erection of a two-family building with side variances. All lot owners within a specified distance from our lot were to appear at a hearing to voice their opinion, pro or con.

It snowed heavily the evening of the variance hearing, and I had hoped the weather would discourage them from appearing, but all were present. Many voiced their objection. The board suggested that they should all look at the architectural design and the size of the building. After doing so, the majority conceded and agreed with the opinion of the council for a variance to be granted.

The construction of our home was the beginning of large houses in the area, as most families bought township land and erected lovely homes. It is now one of the most desirable areas in the township.

In those years of segregation, the reason for rezoning the area after receiving our application for a building permit could be assumed as a justifiable denial. In retrospect, the attorney found a way for us to purchase the adjoining lot right from the township without a face-to-face confrontation or revelation of our intent.

In spite of our contempt and bitterness, I admired the indiscriminate consideration of the mayor and the building inspector, but I often wondered who perpetrated the rezoning.

Building at Ellis Parkway

In 1958 my father became seriously ill. I left from Idlewild in mid-November and arrived home, very much to the surprise of the district people, as the news of my intended visit had not been circulated. However, some people told me that they were expecting me. The doctor wasn't quite sure what the problem was with my father. In those days, especially on a small remote island, some doctors would give prescriptions without telling the patient of their illness and would become quite irritable if questioned by a patient who may not be their peer.

Some people depended on various weeds and herbs rather than drugs. Others sought the Obeah man if they believed in evil spirits. Many died from appendicitis and other ailments that could surgically be cured. I made sure of my father's diagnosis. His heart was failing, accompanied by hypertension. He was advised to refrain from hard work and to get plenty of rest. I spent most of my time at home and at the mineral baths, which were only thirty miles away. I stayed two weeks. Mother's illness had not worsened, though she had gained a lot of weight.

My father died in 1960. The district mourned the loss with my family. Two of my brothers and a sister were encouraged to migrate to England so that my mother and other family members could be helped financially because there were other brothers and sisters in Jamaica that were married with children and needed our support, too.

My mother died in January of 1962. Several inches of snow had fallen the night before and Idlewild Airport was closed for two days. When the plane finally took off, it took a long time to gain altitude. All funeral preparations were completed and waiting for my arrival. She was laid to rest in the family plot beside my father on January 7, 1962. The minister of the Chantilly New Testament Church of God joined with the minister of the Davyton Congregational Church as officiators of the ceremony. I tried to hold back the tears, but when the casket was lowered, almost everyone wept loudly with grief. John, Eliza, and George were living in England and unable to attend the funeral. She had raised us as God had taught her, giving of her best with a smile until she breathed her last breath. There were several well-wishers who offered tributes for the life of Mother Smikle and for the good she had done. I never wipe my tears, but I choked back the sounds of grief while others cried aloud in sad relief. My mother had prayed for me to carry on the wishes of our father in caring for each other, as they had done for us all their lives.

My flights to and from Jamaica were always pleasurable, listening to tourists tell of the lovely time they'd enjoyed there. When asked about the country and the locations of pleasure, I failed to give a satisfactory description; I knew very little about the island. It was winter and, with a week to spare, I decided to visit Montego Bay for the first time.

Upon arriving, I drove around the city, making several observations, then checked into the Holiday Inn for two days in order to gain some experience of what tourism was all about. After my first costly order, I was careful to look at the cost of my meals and drinks. The gratuity was more than I could afford, not to mention the cost of the meals. The dining areas were luxuriously decorated with flowers, and the guests were seated indiscriminately. Swimming and other sports were being enjoyed by blacks and whites alike without any form of discrimination. At night, whites were observed in the company of the native blacks as they danced the limbo and cheered the entertainers, influenced by the spirit of rum punch and other exotic drinks. With my Jamaican accent no one asked where I was from, and they all seemed comfortable enjoying my company. They adopted the native motto, "No problem, Mon."

In spite of the excitement, I missed having Estelle by my side to share the fun. I couldn't help wondering whether those whites practiced discrimination at home, after seeing their behavior on the island, and observed what a difference a vacation made. The breeze from the Caribbean filled my lungs and changed my feelings. I was beginning to fall in love with Jamaica, the country of my birth.

The country had received its independence from Britain. Bauxite, the country's largest export, was being mined within two miles from the Davyton district and employed many people from all over the country. Tremendous improvements in home buildings, the development of new roads and schools, and the accumulation of automobiles were the evidence of its progress.

In the United States, I arranged sponsorship of my daughter and two of my sisters and their families. Women who had no jobs were encouraged to seek domestic work in the United States. Within New Jersey and New York areas, wealthy and professional families with children were happy to use some of the women I recommended.

I have always wanted to help the less fortunate, so I was happy to help many of my nieces and nephews receive their high school educations in the United States. It gave me great satisfaction to see them using the opportunities that they would never be able to afford in Jamaica.

I encouraged education, as in the case of three Jamaicans who lived with us at various times while attending universities in the United States. Two of the young men were the first black students to work at Johns Manville plant, at Manville, while on summer vacation. They received that opportunity when I asked my supervisor to help them. I had observed many white students over the years coming in during the summer and earning a lot of money. They were given a lot of overtime, in all kinds of jobs, which they never refused. Having a summer job saved a lot of time looking for one. One of the young men graduated from Tuskegee with a degree in Veterinary Medicine, the other from Wisconsin State.

There was also a young lady who wanted to come to the United States and attend Columbia, but her mother was reluctant to encourage her. On one of my visits to Jamaica she asked for my help and advice. My wife agreed that she could live with us while attending Columbia. She stayed with us for one year, then joined a New York University friend she knew who was living in New York City. During the summer she worked and earned enough to pay her

B.S. in Chemistry. My wife and I invited her mother and sister from Jamaica so that they could be with her on that glorious day of graduation.

Most of my relatives who joined me in the United States lived within three miles from my home in Edison. On regular summer holidays, my secluded backyard was the scene of many festivities and cookouts. Between eighty and one hundred relatives and friends gathered to enjoy the Jamaican curried goat, rice, peas, jerk chicken, and jerk pork, with lots of soft drinks for the young people and rum punch, Strong Back, and Irish Moss for the adults. The calypso music, blended with popular jazz, made those occasions memorable events.

Under the Urban Renewal program, all the houses at Potters' Crossing were being demolished so that a new development program could be implemented. Under the law, families who lost their homes had to be relocated, and all new plans had to meet the approval of the governing organizations, including the North Edison Civic Improvement Association. The urban renewal met several postponements when plans submitted by nearsighted developers were not approved by the committee. The association wanted an integrated development: low-income homes interspersed with higher income homes and a senior citizens complex, with special consideration for blacks from the area. Some developers wanted separate areas for low income in order to maintain the value of the higher income homes. I was a member of the Mayor Advisory Committee, and the controversy dragged on with frustration and anger for years. Finally a plan was approved which included most of the submitted recommendations. The community center was named in memory of the only black social worker at the time, Minny Bell Veal, who had served the underprivileged children in the area most of her life. The park was named in memory of the president of the North Edison Civic Improvement Association, whose name was James Elder.

The name of the area was changed from the blighted "Potters Crossing" to "North Edison"; the new elementary school was named in memory of Martin Luther King, Jr. Later on a section of the development was named in memory of Robert Holmes, an activist for civil rights.

The North Edison Civic Improvement Association continued their active struggle for civil rights. We embraced and supported the Metuchen and Edison branch of CORE, under

James Farmer, and started to demonstrate and picket businesses that employed no blacks. Rahway's White Castle was targeted, in spite of threats from nightriders who threw rocks or occasional Molotov cocktails at the picketers. Picketing continued under the protection of law enforcement in the area. The annex to the Elizabeth Courthouse was under construction and was targeted for picketing by blacks. That resulted in the arrest of several demonstrators when cement trucks could not deliver materials. The march on Washington in August of 1963 had buses from our area sponsored by the North Edison Civic Improvement Association, CORE, and the NAACP.

I am a member of Bethel Presbyterian Church in Plainfield N.J., having joined in 1957. I held office as Deacon, Elder, Chairman of Stewardship, member of the Committee on Ministry of the Elizabeth Presbytery, President of Bethel Presbyterian Men, and member of the choir. The Presbytery of Elizabeth, which is the center of the Presbyterian Churches in the area, requested that my wife and I join with other Presbyterians from the surrounding area to organize a new Presbyterian Church under the sponsorship of the First Presbyterian Church of Metuchen. Out of that decision the Oak Tree Presbyterian Church was born and we became charter members. The first minister was the Reverend Robert Seaman. He was very instrumental in encouraging desegregation. Many churches in the area sponsored young black students from Mississippi into black and white homes in Edison and Metuchen. That movement took place after many lynchings and the murder of a young black student, Emmett Till, killed by Mississippi racists. The action was taken to show support and compassion and also to support the civil rights movement.

I helped to organize a social club, consisting of ten Jamaicans and four Americans, called the Gibraltar Social Club, which had members from Middlesex, Union, and Somerset counties. We donated most of the money from our dances and bus and boat rides to CORE and the NAACP.

Gibraltar Social Club

May 1963

CHECK FOR A CAUSE—John Elfenbein, left, fund-raising chairman of CORE, holds part f a $300 check presented to Willie F. Williams, center, chairman of the Middlesex County Chapter of CORE, by Wilbert Smikle, president of the Gibraltar Social Club. The club, which held benefit dance to secure the funds, also presented the Somerville branch of the NAACP with a $300 check.

Back on the job, one of the machine tenders died after a short illness. The rumor was that he had lung cancer. He had been a heavy smoker, never wore a dusk mask, and was constantly having trouble with his machine, which created a lot of dust and fumes.

I was given a new position on the job as a Relief Operator of the #4 machine in the cutting and packaging area. The job specified that within an eighthour shift, the six men who work on the machine must each be given fifteen minutes relief from the operation every two hours, three times daily. This was to begin after the first two hours of work. The rest of time was to be used to supply wrapping material for the area. The job called for patience, diplomacy, and good nature. If someone overstayed his time, even only two minutes, it became very difficult to complete my job within the allowed time. To make matters worse, those men had to be given a bathroom break when the occasion became necessary. I continued in the Relief Operator's job for many years and gained much respect for my performance.

The most important job in the cutting and packaging area was that of Cutter Operator. As Relief Operator, I relieved the Cutter Operator also. The Cutter Operator was a very large white man with twenty years of seniority. He died suddenly and the Cutter Operator position was given to me since I had the seniority and the qualifications. The job was less strenuous, but carried more responsibility. Every shingle had to meet the underwriter's requirement. I also had to maintain the required speed and the cooperation of the crew of eight men, six of whom were white.

I was the first black ever to achieve the position of Cutter Operator. My aim was to obtain the top job in the department: machine tender of the prestigious #4 machine. This was a highly respected position and paid the highest salary. The man who held that job was considered "Top Man."

A successful machine tender must have the cooperation of all who work with him on the operation. The machine must maintain constant running speed and very little break down in order to produce good quality material. Operation could be easily sabotaged by one or more dissatisfied workers, thus making it impossible for a machine tender to meet the required quota set forth by the company. Such a machine tender would be removed.

The top machine tender on my shift was an Italian man called Rocky. He was strong, tough, and rugged, and carried a small stogie in the corner of his mouth. His face was always covered with black dust from constant exposure to the dusty areas and asphalt fumes, and with his red lips he looked like a clown. He spoke with an accent and called me "Ju-ma-kee."

Two top tenders died within a few years. They were suspected of having breathing problems. Our machine tender, the tough Rocky, also became ill and died after several months. It was shocking to see how much weight he lost during his illness. His job was posted, and no one with higher seniority or qualifications submitted their name except me and another white man with less seniority. After several days I was summoned to the office of the superintendent who managed the department. He looked at me with apprehension and said loudly, "Do you really want the job?"

"Yes sir," I said.

"Those men will hang you," he countered.

I looked around, making sure that no one was listening, and said, "I can learn that job."

"What I want is production," he answered. "I will give you one month to prove it. The men who you will be working with don't have to like you to do their job, but you certainly have to develop a change of attitude. I remember your encounter a few years ago."

He told me to report for training the following Monday morning at 6 AM to a white tender who was paid 20 percent above my salary to teach me the operation. There were no manuals or plans available for me to study. Hundreds of switches for various machines were located all over different areas and were very confusing to a new learner. My instructor was touching switches from panels that had several inoperable ones, which should have been removed. Some switches on the first floor operated machines on the second floor, where tanks containing various mixtures were stored. My instructor refused to explain the details of the operations to me, and when I asked him he snapped and said, "I ain't showin' you a damn thing." To report the matter would have been a grave mistake.

The next day I bought a notebook, and as I followed him around, I made sketches of all the areas and the locations of all the various switches, the machines they activated, and the services rendered. I made diagrams identifying all the valves and the work they performed. As I followed my instructor, the faces of the white men were unfriendly as they gazed at me. They knew I would be their leader, and if I failed, the job would be re-posted and I would never be given a second chance. I was determined to prove my ability to do the job and also to gain their cooperation and respect.

On my third week, I was scheduled to start operations beginning first shift on Monday morning. Alone, I had to prepare the machines and have everything ready when the other workers arrived at 7 AM.

The most respected fellow was a large, cigar-smoking Pole named Ray. He had about twenty years of seniority and looked forward to succeeding Rocky. Ray hated problems. His job was to watch the asphalt as it was applied to the passing paper, making sure that the right granules and dust were applied. Though I prepared the machine, the one thing I feared was starting it up, which required skill and knowledge.

My instructor made sure I never had the chance to execute that very important procedure. The main switch which started the machine is a lever which had to be touched gently so that the motors, which had several speeds, were synchronized to prevent the paper on the loop frame from snapping and breaking, which would cause asphalt and granules to spill over the area, resulting in waste, cleanup time, and an accumulation of fumes and dust. I asked Ray to do the start-up for me, reminding him that I got the job only because no one in his area had applied for it. He didn't answer me, but when the time came, I gave the signal and he began to operate the starter switch while I applied the asphalt and granules and kept a keen eye on the process. All the other men responded to their duties as the operation gained speed. Ray returned to his bench while I checked the specifications and performed other responsibilities, much to the surprise of all the whites in this crucial area.

Once the operation was going smoothly, a machine tender had a little free time to make observations and share communications. I gave short breaks to the men for coffee, a favor seldom offered by Rocky.

It was most unusual for a new machine tender to be scheduled to start-up on the first shift on Monday morning, when there were three shifts. Usually they would take over the second or third shift when the operation was well in progress and there were fewer chances for problems. It was important that I be very diplomatic in taking over the start-up job from Ray because he had gained the respect of his peers and was the top man.

During an eight-hour shift, the machine had to be stopped for reasons such as problems in the cutting and packaging areas or to change defective parts or motors. I was finally able to manage the process by slowing down or speeding up the machine when the occasion allowed, or by running the machine at a slow rate of speed without asphalt or granules on the surface of the paper, which is called a "dry run." Overcoming the fear to perform that very important task was a credit I attributed to Ray. He finally yielded the start-up procedure to me and was satisfied with my ability to perform the task.

It took approximately forty-five minutes to fully prepare the machines for start-up on a typical Monday morning. First, all steam valves had to be opened to supply heat to the main asphalt pit and all other areas, making sure they were maintained at the required temperatures. All water and air valves had to be checked for blockages. Motors on both floors had to be functioning as well as the granules and color displacement areas, and all operators had to be in their respective areas, ready to perform their duties. The machine tender was also responsible for a full, written, daily production report to the company. Production records were posted daily, and each machine tender tried to beat the record of his peer. There were times when I suspected foul play when a machine suddenly broke down. I never allowed those incidents to spoil my good humor. We would quickly clean the area and repair the damage for a speedy continuation of the operation.

Ray went on vacation and, in his absence, the operation continued without interruption. I was now the top man in the department, and the warmth and appreciation of my black coworkers was clearly demonstrated by their enthusiasm and respect. The white workers realized they had to accept the inability of blacks as a myth, as many blacks were able to achieve top jobs throughout the plant.

After five years I started to have breathing problems, especially when running with friends. I had worn a dusk mask at all times in areas that were hazardous with dust and fumes, but the condition worsened—but whenever I vacationed in Jamaica, my breathing would improve considerably.

After twenty-five years I was inducted into the Quarter Century Club, which gave an elaborate celebration to honor more than two hundred and fifty employees and their spouses. Each employee was given a gift of sentimental value. The wives were given corsages and other flowers and commendation for their patience in putting up with and caring for us over the many years. There was lots of kissing and hugging and hand shaking. Blacks and whites joked and made fun of each other in what seemed to be brotherly love.

The following day it was back to the grindstone. Production was all that mattered; the kind words of yesterday just fuel for tomorrow's speed.

My foreman was a large Polish man who weighed approximately three hundred pounds. He sometimes reminded me of the Jamaican who tried to ship a box of snow back to Jamaica. He never showed any kindness towards me, nor did he care too much for blacks in general. When overtime became available, he had his favorites, mostly whites, and for that reason I had to issue a few grievances against him for unfair labor practices. In spite of our differences, there was mutual respect between us. I admired his ambition in making sure his only son, whom he would often brag about, became a jet fighter pilot. His son came to visit him on the job one day in his shining uniform, looking handsome and proud. He was leaving for Vietnam, and many of the whites surrounded him and shook his hand and wished him a safe return.

I got close for a good look at him. His father introduced him to me, and he shook my hand and smiled. In spite of the injustices to blacks, especially in the south, his smile stayed with me, and I was choked with grief when news came two months later that he was missing in action over Vietnam.

I finally convinced Estelle to fly with me to Jamaica, but not without the help of our friend Mary, who accompanied us. We had been married for almost twenty years and had spent a lot of our vacations together throughout the United States and Canada. The thought of being in the air made her nervous, but with Mary along, her fears seemed to be relieved.

On Sunday, February 15, 1970, we left Kennedy Airport for a three-week tour of Jamaica. It was a very cold and snowy morning. We boarded Air Jamaica at 10:30 AM, but didn't leave until noon because the plane had to be de-iced. The captain welcomed us aboard and apologized for the delay. To make us feel happy he told us the temperature in Montego Bay was eighty-six degrees. We arrived in Kingston at 5:15 PM, after briefly stopping in Montego Bay. The flight was smooth and the stewardesses gave a lovely fashion show on the way down, much to the delight of Estelle and Mary, who seldom missed fashion shows given by their own Key Women's Club. It was an exciting experience for Estelle and Mary as they greeted my relatives and friends in my own hometown of Davyton.

My brother David had a large farm with yams, bananas, and navel oranges and a variety of hibiscus, roses, and bougainvilleas which, blended with the songs of birds, gave the picture of a tropical paradise. The morning sun greeted us with a temperature of seventy degrees, gradually rising to eighty or eighty-six, tempered by the gentle breeze from the blue Caribbean, about forty miles away. The nights were cool and comfortable, but were interrupted by the crowing of roosters and crickets.

Mandeville, the capital, had many attractive stores, an open market, and good bargains in jewelry, clothes, and gifts. I tried not to interfere, but resented the constant confirmation from the women to "keep the change."

We attended Davyton United Church and received a warm welcome by the congregation. When introduced by the minister, some of the older folks enquired whether I was the boy who they called "Mr. Man" from many years ago.

The native foods of *ackee* and *saltfish*—along with curried goat, rice, and peas—were always a warm welcome for dinner, not to mention the pepper pot soup and steamed fish. Our time was spent between David's home and Miss Sewell's, at Williamsfield. Her sister had sponsored me from England.

We were invited by Mrs. Mitchell to spend a few days at her home in Crofts Hill in Clarendon. Her daughter Hermine was the first student to live at our home while she attended Columbia University. Crofts Hill is a small plateau among the hills of southeast Clarendon. The people are friendly and warm. On our way to Crofts Hill, we heard songs along the narrow roadway. Farmers formed groups and worked together on each other's farm as the time to prepare for planting drew near. They blended their voices in harmony, and from a distance they sounded like an angelic choir. Early one morning at Crofts Hill, my wife heard the braying of a donkey from a nearby farm. What she saw hanging from that male donkey prompted her to get her camera. On her return, the "scene" had disappeared. All she ended up getting was a few hee-haws. We all wondered what she would have done with the pictures.

We left Crofts Hill and headed for Montego Bay, our next destination. We cruised through the small mountain roads, dodging large trucks and buses as we headed toward the north coast highway, which is one of the country's largest roads. It runs along the coastline and is nicely kept with shrubberies and other attractive flowers and plants.

We stopped at Discovery Bay, an historical center where Christopher Columbus first landed when he discovered the island in 1494. Many of the exhibits are originals from that time. The area is decorated with flowers and artifacts, and food and rest are provided. Tourists can be seen enjoying the blue refreshing water of the bay. Along the way to Montego Bay are old Spanish buildings whose names have not changed, such as Rhino Beano and Terre Nuevo, just to name a few.

We arrived at Montego Bay in the early evening and checked into the Casa Montego Hotel. We were welcomed with rum punch. The ladies were too modest to accept a second, but David and I didn't turn down any extras that were offered.

The rooms had a clear view of the famous Doctor's Cave Beach, a short distance away. We listened to the internationally famous Song Birds and the dynamic Blair Sisters at the Club Royal Box. We also heard the famous folk singer Keith Stewart at Club Yellow. At the Banana Club, we all tried to do the limbo, but the joke was on me as I fell on my back many times.

David, who had come with us to Montego Bay, had to return to work after three days. I drove from Montego Bay to Kingston, stopping at picturesque Dun's River Falls in Ochos Rios, and through the rainforest gorge of Fern Gully.

Dun's River Falls

The road was treacherous and winding with lots of hills overlooking deep gullies, especially around Mount Diablo and Mount Rushmore.

We made a stop at Linstead to get a glimpse of the famous Linstead Market. It was at that market the famous native calypso blues song was written:

"Carry mi ackee go a Linstead Market
not a quatty wot sell,
Oh wat a day wat a night
not a quatty wot sell."

Estelle and Mary wanted to take pictures of that area since they'd heard that tune from us many times. Our next stop and final destination was the Sheraton Hotel in Kingston, the capital of the island. There had been quite a lot of improvements; the grounds were covered with beautiful flowers, and several lounges had been added, and top entertainers made our visit there most unforgettable. There was a show at the Ward Theatre, a portrayal of the moon landing, which was very beautifully done.

The ladies had fun buying jewelry and perfumes at the local craft markets. We toured the famous Hope Botanical Gardens and the Castleton Garden, finally heading up to Red Hills to get the most picturesque view of the city of Kingston.

The evening before our departure, the Sheraton management gave a great party for all the guests, which concluded a memorable vacation. The return flight was smooth most of the way, with the exception of a moment of disturbance, which didn't seem to bother Estelle.

We landed at JFK and my daughter, with a few of her friends greeted us with a warm welcome. Estelle was pleased and decided she would not miss any more trips. She had fallen in love with Jamaica and its people, especially the school children in their various uniforms and their exceptionally good manners.

Before leaving Jamaica, we had invited the minister of Davyton Church to spend a vacation with us in the United States. He was the first black minister to be highly recognized by the congregation and had never taken a vacation. Three months later he became ill and was advised to take a leave from his job. He and his wife and two sons spent two to three weeks with us. It was their first visit, and the experience was rewarding. He was able to tour New York City, including the United Nations building and the theatre district, and Washington, DC. At a party given in his honor, he met many friends and expressed his thanks to God.

Retirement

Just before the end of 1979, the company offered an early retirement proposal to employees sixty years of age or older. It was considered a once-in-a-lifetime offer and carried a cash lump sum payoff and a lifetime monthly pension. The union embraced the offer, although it was rumored that it was orchestrated to get rid of the older men with seniority that were slowing down, in anticipation of a slow down in production.

I was sixty years old and welcomed the opportunity to retire with full pension at a time when my health was failing. The option would end on December 31, 1979. Within 2 years, I would be eligible for social security.

My desire to help my family was foremost in my thoughts. Sharing my time, talents, and resources had given me fulfillment.

Estelle and Wilbert

Estelle became ill in 1954. In September 1955, surgery was performed on her at Rahway Memorial Hospital. She remained in good health and was active in many community programs. She was a member of the Oak Tree Presbyterian Church and served as a Sunday school teacher. She was secretary of the Key Women's Club and joined the North Edison Civic Improvement Association, the NAACP, CORE, and the Edison- Metuchen Race Relation Council in the fight for civil rights. She helped to organize the march on Washington in August 1963 in support of Martin Luther King, Jr. She was a lover of children, especially those that were mentally challenged. She resigned from her job with Emerson Cool (an air conditioner maker) in order to work with the handicapped children of the Union County Day School.

She received awards from the citizen's group of the school for her devotion and compassion. She loved entertainment and traveling and was a loving wife, blessed with strong moral values, who always stood firmly behind me. She was my "ideal." She died of cancer in August of 1985 after a short illness.

> *"God gave her skill in comfort art; he set her apart unto a life of love and sympathy. She shares the weight of ill in many broken hearts and with a smile which only Christ can give."*

The Family Reunion
August 1988

During the Christmas of 1987, at my home in New Jersey, a few of the family members held a meeting and decided to have a family reunion in our native Jamaica. I was asked to organize the occasion for August, 1988, and the following arrangements were made.

August 18	Family members from Jamaica, the United States, Canada, and England meet for a special day of renewal and reunion.
August 19	A grand picnic to be held with an open invitation to the community for all to join in the celebration.
August 21, 11AM	A special service of Thanksgiving at the Davyton United Church at 11 AM, and the church of our late parents at 7 PM.
August 21, 7PM	A special service of Thanksgiving at the New Testament Church of God in Chantily. *Note: A special financial contribution to both churches will be made by the Smikle family to help in their religious activities.*

Within the first three months of 1988, all known Smikles were notified and invited to join in the celebration. Group tickets at low rates were secured for those abroad who would travel together, making sure each person chose the return date of their choice.

The area north of the old homestead, which was newly acquired, was selected and the ground prepared. A large temporary kitchen was erected on the picnic grounds to shelter the grills in case of rain. The Jamaica 3rd Battalion offered their support in erecting two large tents. All tables and chairs were made available by the Davyton United Church. A local band and a D.J. were hired to provide musical entertainment. The menu was prepared by some of the district's best cooks and consisted of curried goat with rice and peas, jerk pork, jerk chicken, roast beef, macaroni, yams, boiled dumplings, string beans, carrots, salad, Manish water, various drinks for adults, and soft drinks for children and fair ladies.

The sons and daughters of Joseph and Ellen Smikle: John, the first, followed by Irene, Wilbert, Anita, David, Nelvy, Ruth, Eliza, George, and Imogene, joined with all other family relatives in welcoming each other and the community of Davyton to a great celebration, giving thanks to God. The occasion was blessed by the oldest member of the church, Uncle Don, followed by the minister of Davyton United.

Smikle Family Reunion, August 1988

Smikle Family Reunion, August, 1988

Smikle Family Reunion, August, 1988
(After church)

Conclusion

Four dreams from my youthful days have been fulfilled. Each carried me through God's chartered paths to jobs known only to Him.

He showed me sceneries long before their existence and beyond my imagination. The words and music of these dreams came from the transformation of my thoughts as I was lifted up in the midst of these places, which were revealed.

The building top of Fort Simmons was revealed before its existence. The large field of asparagus of South Jersey was also shown to me before my first trip to America. The pile of brick from the destroyed city was seen of London before it happened. That twinkling light from the eastern sky of Jamaica was later observed as a jumbo jet.

My fifth dream of the babe in the cradled arms of his mother, seen from the eastern sky, with a beckoning finger to me, is a constant reminder of "God's Divine Calling."

Glossary

Backra	Land baron
Bassider tree	Tree with slim, tender limbs that don't break easily
Busha	Field hand supervisor, Uncle Tom
CORE	Congress Of Racial Equality
Custorlurium	Official appointed by the Governor General and is similar to a notary public
Detol	A deodorizing ingredient
Guango Tree	Short shade tree that does not attract lightning due to its height
Lasse	Machete
Locust	A form of the tamarind fruit
NAACP	National Association for the Advancement of Colored People
Pus	Cat

Quadrille	A dance like the jitterbug done with four couples
Rose applies	Crab apples
Sankey	Small hymnal book
Set Goozou	Cast a spell
Stooge	Snitch
Strong back	A drink made from roots and herbs
Wackle	A form of wicker

This book answers the question *Who is that man?* and, furthermore, brings enlightenment and recognition of the free services that are being rendered by voluntary groups of Jamaicans and foreigners in the remote areas.

It is my wish, as the author, to express the mystery of God's guidance in my life through dreams and to inspire all to seek God's power and will in their struggles to succeed in good commitments.

I was born in the rugged mountain district of Manchester, Jamaica, West Indies. The third of nine children of humble farm parents, I attended the local elementary school, and after graduation, continued to study for the first and second year pupil-teacher's examinations. At the age of twenty, I attended a government Practical Training Center, supposedly for sixteen- and seventeen-year-old boys. I studied farming and woodwork for three years.

With a strong desire to uplift the family's standard of living, I took the opportunity to travel to the United States to work on farms under the U.S. War Food Administration program during World War II.

Returning to Jamaica after the war, I worked in Kingston for a short time, then migrated to England in 1947. I immigrated to the United States in 1948 and resided in New Jersey, becoming a citizen in 1954. That same year I became a civil rights activist and fought in the struggle for the next twenty years. A Presbyterian with a strong religious faith in God, I married one of Maryland's most beautiful in 1951. She was called to glory after thirty-one years. The father of two daughters, I married my second wife in 1996. I retired from my first job after thirty-one years of service.

I rebuilt the Haynes' old homestead in Jamaica and called it "The Davyton House." It is used on occasion by groups doing voluntary dental work in the community for school children and others who are unable to pay.

I resided in Jamaica occasionally during 1990-1995 for health reasons. In 1993, a secret investigation was conducted by the law enforcement authorities of the area to determine my identity after I was visited by the then Governor General of Jamaica, his Excellency, Sir Howard Cooke.